Options After Foreclosure

Faith Based Solutions to Foreclosure

By Tris

Mustard Seed Works, Inc.

Franklin, MI

Published by Mustard Seed Works, Inc.

Options After Foreclosure is a trademark of
Mustard Seed Works Inc
Edited by Barbra Baker
Cover design by Austin & Paris Designs
Printed in the U.S.A.

To order this title, and others please contact
www.TradePostEarth.com
800-738-7712

Mustard Seed Works, Inc., P.O. Box 70
Franklin, MI 48025
www.mustardseedworks.com

ISBN: 978-0-615-19532-2

Library of Congress Control Number: 2008924262

ACKNOWLEDGMENTS

I happily take this opportunity to thank God for his wonderful blessings in my life. I am grateful for his patience and love. To Him, be all honor and glory.

I thank God for my granny, who prayed for me, when I didn't have the sense to pray for myself. For my mom who loved me, when I thought I was unlovable. For my siblings who stood by me, when I could not stand up for myself. For my man who made be believe that I was beautiful and worthy of love. For my children who allowed God's love to flow through them and fill me with joy.

Finally, I thank God for my true friends, who laughed with me, when I laughed, cried when I cried, and prayed for me all along the way for peace.

Options After Foreclosure

Contents

Preface

Today my children asked me about the Lord. They wanted to know what was "one day" to the Lord. As I thought about my answer, something occurred that I never really considered before. A day to the Lord is more like 1000 years, to us (Psalms 90:4). So when God says "yes" to our prayers, and asks us to wait, He does not necessarily mean in our time, but in His.

When we pray, God is listening. He hears His children, and does answer us, and the answer is yes. When I tell my kids yes, it means yes we can do it or buy it, or see it, but sometime in the near future. Maybe tomorrow, or the next day, but yes we can.

God works in His own time, and many times, he means yes, but not right now. We wait and wait, but those who are weak, begin to doubt God, thinking that He has forgotten them, or said no to their petition.

For those who truly trust the Lord, they know to be patient so when God tells us to wait, he expects that we will not grow faint. He begins working right then to make the way as He promised in His word. If you remember Jesus said, "That whatever you ask in my name will be granted" (John 14:13).

With your foreclosure, your business, your life, your family, finances whatever, trust God and hold on. He heard your prayers and has already begun moving things in accordance. Sometimes it just may take a little longer, than one would imagine, to realize the answer to a prayer, but baby, you had better know from the moment a child of God releases a prayer, and plants the seed, the answer is one its way.

True we are but mere mortals and telling you to hold on in the face of foreclosure is easy for me to say, but I have done it myself. Actually, in my circumstances, the loss of my house allowed the Lord open a wonderful window. I realized that it was not the end of the world, but the beginning of a new adventure, and it surely was not my last house.

This is not your last house either, that is if you trust Him. He has so much in store for His children, and as you do the things He requires, seeking to please Him, you will be amazed at the life He will provide, fulfilling the deepest desires of your heart.

Tris

Procedures for Michigan

Before we begin, I want to be sure that you understand five very important facts regarding your possible foreclosure. If after reading this book you find that you are unable, or unwilling to find a solution to save the relationship between you and your mortgage company, please be aware of the following rights.

1. You have until the day of the sheriff sale to find a way to save your home by making an arrangement, file bankruptcy or whatever.
2. The court is the only entity that can legally evict you from your home.
3. You should not move out of the house, without notifying the mortgage company, to do so is considered abandonment.
4. The IRS counts your foreclosure as income.
5. God loves you no matter what you do.

God loves you, no matter what you do, so be of "good cheer", even in the midst of confusion. Yes, your home is in jeopardy, but that probably means it is time for change.

The foreclosure is a symptom of a fair bigger problem, so now we must determine what is causing your problem, and hopefully this book and the accounts of people just like you will help to find a way to make adjustments necessary to cure your problem.

So let us rehash what we learned thus far, if any person, other than a sheriff or other court appointed officer comes to your door without written authorization from the court, a "writ", attempting to evict you, it is considered illegal and you should immediately call the police.

Should that illegal attempt include the unauthorized removal of your things from the property, or the tampering with the utilities, immediately call the police, and sue the violator in small claims court.

Even though the house went through foreclosure, in Michigan your official date to be out of the house comes from the court. The court clerk will send you a letter of eviction that states, "move by this date or come to court."

Should you need more time to move, go to court? Ensure that you arrive 15 minutes before the time indicated on the summons. Once you stand before the judge, or meet with the attorney who is representing the mortgage company, humbly ask for an additional 30 days.

The courts realize that if you had abandoned the home without first notifying the mortgage company, would have left the house vulnerable for the local vandals. Those thieves can come in and strip a house bare, in a matter of hours, making the naked house then is worth considerably less to the mortgage company, and therefore they want to work with you hand in hand to cause a smooth transition. Long story short the attorneys generally, do not object to the judge allowing you additional time to move.

Don't forget you want the mortgage company to yield as much as possible with the sale of your house, because you will be responsible for the difference in the amount you owe and the amount for which the property brings at the sheriff's sale. You should also note that the difference will count as income to you, and you will be assessed a tax of which you will have to pay unless you make the appropriate adjustments on your tax return.

Lastly, and most importantly, I live in the great state of Michigan and, therefore, the rules and procedures discussed in this manual reflect the foreclosure process for that area. You must conduct your own additional research for your state.

Use the principles contained within this book to direct your research into the specific procedures for the state in which your property is located. If you have questions, ask them, call any lawyer in the yellow pages and ask your general question, they do not charge you for that.

My daddy always told me not to simply accept what somebody tells me, unless it comes directly from the source, and then, still ask questions. Always check things out for yourself, after all, information is relative to time, and things change daily.

Use my information as a springboard for further investigation, and discover for yourself the limitations specific to your situation. In other words, this information is not be used in place of an attorney, but merely as a means of possibilities. I am merely reporting to you facts of specific events regarding foreclosures that I have personally observed, or experienced.

Okay, now that I have protected myself, and hopefully have given you a bit of peace, at the same time, lets get into it point by point, so you can begin to create your plan using the options after the foreclosure.

A friend of mine has a picture in her living room of a man who has made it over the wall, and rather than running on with his glorious new life, he stops just long enough to reach back and pull someone else over the very same wall. Consider this my hand, to help you over a wall in your life.

1

You Are Not Alone

"I am with you always"
Matthew 28:20

You think that the bank wants to take your house. Wrong! The bank actually wants nothing to do with the ownership of your house. They just want to know that you intend to pay them, as agreed.

They would much prefer some kind of arrangement to receive a reasonable amount of the mortgage payment that ultimately will lead to their only goal, getting back the money they loaned you to buy your house in the first place.

The real questions are:

1. Do you really know what it is you actually want?
2. Have you really tired to save your relationship with the mortgage company?
3. Have you spoken to the retention and mitigation departments?
4. Have you told them what it is you really want?
5. Have you offered a partial payment so that they know you are not consciously trying to default on your commitment?
6. Most importantly, are you applying active prayer, followed by effort driven faith?

You need to get angry. If you are truly a child of God, then you should understand that you have the power to make a thing change. Your faith can cause the mortgage company to work with you, and it does not matter if you already have received the notice of the sheriff sale date. You have only to desire, and believe. Buy yourself time, do whatever you need to do, but save your home, if of course, that is in line with God's will.

Foreclosure today is as common as the word help. There are so many people caught in this situation, and they are embarrassed to ask for help. They don't realize that they are not alone. In 2007, Wayne County Michigan posted an average of 2000 new foreclosures for that county alone, every 30 days. In other parts of the county, the rates are even higher like in Arizona where they are posting an average of 3000 foreclosures a month.

The number of foreclosures across America has reached such a high peak that financial analysts have deemed it of "tsunami" proportions. No baby, you are defiantly not alone.

Families across America are sweating month after month, dodging the bullet of foreclosure. Once dual income households with bills paid on time every month are now struggling as their income is "chopped" in half. Those who once had suitable monies put away for a rainy day have depleted their savings trying to survive, in the wake of increased unemployment.

At one time, people flocked to Michigan as the auto industry guaranteed jobs. People came from all over the country, able to find jobs in the plants or in one of the thousands of businesses that supported the industry.

People have tired to blame the governor, but I say that this was something that is beyond her control. Technology is the real villain, reducing what once employed 500 workers down to 50 employees. The 50 remaining jobs do no more than to support and repair the computers and robots that replaced their past co-workers. It is like something out of an Orson Wells nightmare.

The companies that once hired millions have had to cut their headcounts over, and over again. As General Motors, Ford, and Chrysler struggle to remain profitable, at one time or another, each company has had to lay off massive numbers of people, leaving employees to collect 26 weeks of unemployment with little hope of local employment. Again, I state that you are not alone.

So as a "Child of God", what do you do to survive? How do you maintain in the reality of lack? Is everyone in lack? Isn't it funny, that while so many are without the finances of yesterday, there are still a whole lot of people doing exceptionally well?

I state that regardless of what is going on all around you, if you are in the place intended for you, fulfilling your purpose, then God can and will make a way out of no way. Many of those people who are doing well may just be in the position intended for His purposes. While others are working for the other side, and reaping the temporary benefits of "selling ones soul".

This is not a Bible lesson, but a time to see truth, so check out II Kings 6, and read how a man of faith made the seemingly impossible, become possible. A man of God was working with a borrowed axe; the axe-handle broke, dropping the head into the water, below them. Someone without faith would reason the weight of the iron in the axe-head, would make it fall to bottom of the lake. The man of faith knew that by reaching, trying with faith, to make a thing so, can cause change beyond understanding.

In the verse, the man of God, in faith, reached for the axe-head, stretching as far as he could toward the goal, and finally his faith caused the axe-head to swim or float toward him. When the axe-head was close enough to grab, he told the others around him to grab it, and they did.

Think about your house as that axe-head falling into the river below you. Iron is heavy and generally sinks right to the bottom, but faith makes it float, just as you can save your own home, if you would only reach, stretch, and try.

It is up to you to cause change in your life. Make the iron swim in your own life, have faith. Live beyond your own understanding. Get angry, and let that anger steer-up your faith in you so that you can make the mortgage company work with you to save your home. Cause some change now while the water around you is troubled.

There is a story in the bible that talks about a pool of water, that the angels would visit once a year. When they visited they would stir, or trouble the water, and then the first one in this "troubled water" would be changed, or relieved of whatever was ailing him.

Right now, you are in the middle of a storm, your own troubled water. Don't run from it, but use it, as your chance, to heal your aliments? Take this chance to change your life. Stand firm and fight for your home. There is peace in the middle of the storm.

Find a way out of the mess that has caused you to get behind, and create a way to keep your home, and then go forward. Consider this trouble your opportunity to change, remember no pain, no gain.

Call up that mortgage company, and demand that they find a way to work out a solution so that both sides can win. Speak to your problems, utilize the workable solutions that God will provide, pay attention.

When I asked the clients coming into my office what had they done to avoid the foreclosure, they looked at me as if I were crazy. Beyond their prayers, they knew not what else to do—that was the same situation for the Jews in Nehemiah 5:2-5. There we see that they too were mortgaged up to their eyeballs, and behind on all payments.

They could not pay their mortgage, little less their taxes, and were forced to borrow monies enough to pay a small portion of their taxes, in order to keep their property. Worse yet, if they did not find a way to borrow the money, they would be forced to sell their children into slavery in order to satisfy their debts.

The man of God saw what was happening, and got angry demanding that the debt be "removed". "Restore" he demanded full of faith, and the creditors said okay (Nehemiah 5:11-12). "Why", because he used his God given power and asked. No one had demanded that the creditors do something different. They let the debt control them rather than controlling it. Speak to the debt, don't ignore the phone calls, speak to your creditors, tell them that you want to keep your home, demand that they make a way for you to resolve that debt, and reinstate your loan.

Recently the major banks decided to enact programs that will allow them to do just that, restore your mortgage. You must ask them about the "Hope Program", or speak to the Retention Department.

Unable to get positive results you may file a chapter 13 bankruptcy that will automatically block the sheriff's sale. Your credit is already a mess, so let's create a winning scenario.

In the next few chapters, we will discuss other options, and how clients have effectively used each one to reach a workable solution to their mountain of a problem called foreclosure.

As believers, we must remember who the sustainer really is, no matter what. The situation does not matter because God will always make a way, out of no way, for his children, that is, if you trust Him.

Trust Him! Those are the words that scroll across on my cell phone and computer screens, as a greeting, reminding me everyday not to focus on what I hear or even see as I walk through this life. Not to look at the things I have done, or left undone, have or don't have, or even how much I owe, but look only to the fact that God loves me and wants my life to be abundantly peaceful, full of happiness, joy, and prosperity. I have to remember that the only thing that matters is that I remain obedient, and sometimes that may just mean closing my eyes, as I stand in the middle of a storm, so that I can allow God to be God.

The knowledge of this allows me to see past the bills, the lack of money in the bank, and even past the bill collectors calling me on the phone. By trusting in the Lord, I know He will bring me to a place where those things are no longer the reality of the present, but remnants from the past. You must declare that same thing in your own life, and then you can begin to save your home.

I am only telling you what I know, because He has done this so many times in the past, over, and over again in my life. When I look back at all the troubles in my life, they in reality were opportunities for me to show God just how much I trusted Him, for joy did come in the morning.

2

Why Me?

"Your faith has healed you" Matthew 9:22

The Shepherd at my church, is a powerful, spirit filled woman, who is proud of the fact that she is a cancer survivor. A smaller person, who is unaware of "whose" they are, might have cried out curses, blaming God for their reality, but not her. Here is a person fully committed to God, using her test as a testimony.

Isn't that interesting, that the word "test" is the beginning of testimony. It is, as if to say, that in order to have a testimony, you must start with a "test". My shepherd is preaching "His" word, and directing souls to salvation, so why did the Lord allow cancer to enter that servant's body?

Undoubtedly, you are asking the same question regarding the "storm" going on in your life. She cannot answer the question of why, but she can tell you that it has helped to bring her closer in helping others of the same affliction. Does it really matter why? As much as understanding that the "why" is in God's purpose for her life? It may just go back to the "test" in testimony. How much more effective is she, as a living example of God's grace, putting her in a better position to help and encourage others?

There is a purpose for everything; nothing happens just by chance, even foreclosure. It could be that the forces are using this as a chance to kill you. Remember in Job, the forces decided to test him by taking away his house, family, and business in hopes that he would curse God and die. It did not happen quite as planned. Actually, in the end, Job received all of the things he had lost and more, because he continued to praise God in spite of the situation.

Could be that your foreclosure, the pastor's cancer, the closing of the plants, are all various types of tests, as in the case of Job? Only God knows what is waiting for you on the other side. My pastor prayed her way through cancer and now is standing on the other side. She is able to cry out praises that are loud enough to encourage anyone else standing behind that very same mountain.

Christ tells us that if we should have faith even as small as a mustard seed, then we can look at any mountain or problem and say "be moved" and it will do just that. For my pastor, the mountain was cancer. Your mountain at this time is obviously your foreclosure. I say "at this time", because it never ends. There will always be a new mountain, a new test, in your way just waiting for you to move it. So buck up, it could be worse.

I used to tell people that all the time, but until I really went out into the world and saw just how bad things could get, did I really believe it? I met people who did curse God in the face of reality, and their lives clearly magnified the result. Please understand as I do, that cursing God does not necessarily mean that you verbally call God names, but you can curse God with the things you do, or leave undone.

There is a passage in the Bible that states, "The man who knows God's laws, but chooses to ignore them, is worse off than a man who never knew God at all." We all sin, and to say otherwise would be a sin within itself. The speed and diligence with which we turn back to the Lord is what keeps our blessings flowing in life.

To curse God would be to know the way and purposely go in the opposite direction, even in the light of the Spirit trying to redirect you. God loves us so much, that He will allow us to do and live just how we want. God will love you all the way down into the gates of hell if that is your will, for your life.

It is equally important that you, as a faithful child, realize that you "shall have whatever you say". So if you started off saying that this was your home and you wanted to pay the house off, yet never took care of it, didn't cut the grass, not making it a home, half paying the note, well you got what your actions portrayed. You should be doing all that you could to keep it, praising God through actions and not just lip service.

From the very day that God gave me my new home, I have believed in my heart that He would allow me to live in this house as long as I wished. I also had the power from God to work hard at my purpose, and I could pay it off in much less than 30 years.

As long as I trusted God, stayed on his path, He would make a way for me to have what I say. I am talking about the house that God gave me after my foreclosure.

Before my present home I lived in Marietta Georgia with my now ex-husband. When I look back to Marietta, I never really considered that home my home. I remember when my granny came to visit me, she commented that it was a nice house for me to raise my children, and she hoped I would turn it into a home. I remember saying that it was only a temporary thing, and "that we would not be there very long". Seven years later we were moving, happily back to Michigan after the foreclosure.

When the foreclosure happened, for a short while, I was sad, thinking what would I do now? My husband had left me and the house was gone, with nothing left but the children and me. That is what I tried to tell myself, but the reality was that God was right there with me, leading me to a new path created for His purpose. I said that we would not be in that house long, and we were not. "You shall have what you say," that is what Christ tells us, and that is what happened.

Now that does not mean that I will not have troubles in my new home. I still have to dodge the foreclosure bullet, but by choosing to obey God, working hard to use my talents for His purpose, trusting in His love, He will continue to make a way for me out of "no-way".

My pastor says that her good days far outweigh her bad days, and that goes for me too. That means that there are bad days, days when I fall back into fear, for no reason until I remember to trust in the Lord. I am still here in my house that I will pay off and leave to my children, I shall have just what I say, Thanks be unto God.

I am telling all of this because foreclosure is nothing but a process, and you have to understand that you have the power to rise above, if that is what you really want. I declare it is up to you because it is your prayers, your work, your ability to control your monies, and your ability to do all that you can to make sure that house stays yours. I know that sounds like a lot of "whoowe", but it is reality.

Words are what God used to create the earth. He said "let there be light," and the sun shined. He created us in His image, and therefore I argue that we have the power to declare a thing and make our words live.

"Anything is possible if you have faith" (Mark 9:23). These are the words spoken by Jesus, so when we make statements, the universe begins to move toward the fulfilling of the command. When you say, it will be all right, baby you are right.

God wants us to talk to Him, pursue His purpose for our lives, and sometimes that just may feel like a long road with no end. One woman in foreclosure said that she thought God had forgotten about her. I wondered if she had forgotten about

Him. Did she bother to thank Him for all the blessings thus far? During the bad times especially, and of course on the good ones, did she thank Him?

The ability to thank God is our weapon against evil. Sounds crazy, but think about it. King David said, "Praise will forever be on my lips." He knew the power of praise even in the face of danger he praised the Lord, and God loved him because of it.

Of course, it is impossible to thank God for all the blessings, there are just too many, to count, it just is not possible. As Steve Harvey, eloquently put it in his imaginary introduction of Jesus, "his accomplishments are too many to list", but trying to thank Him will bring you peace, even in the face of foreclosure and peace will lead you to a plan.

My mother once told me that sometimes when she feels low, with the burden of loving her children, allowing their disappointments to become her own (that is a true test of love), she needs to stop and remember all the of blessings of her life. When these days come, and they do come to all of God's children, she gets out a pen and some paper and starts writing down as many blessing as she can remember. Before long, she is tired of writing and full of joy, as it is simply impossible for her to remember all the many blessings, the ways and means that God has smiled on her life.

There simply is no way possible to list all of the ways that God has blessed your life. I don't mean the car and the house. I mean the blessings beyond the material. The house and the car are nothing more than the result of the blessing.

I am talking about the ability to attend school, to get the degree, to get the job, where you met your husband. I mean the healthy mom who brought you into the world, and guides you with love from the pitfalls of drug addiction. I mean the alcoholic anonymous program where you can find help, connect with someone who is much like you helping to drive you away from the addiction.

My mom's list must have something like the blessing of God allowing her to gain her master's degree, in turn allowed her to get the position that allowed her to put her children through college, laugh with her grandchildren, in addition to also buying the car and the house.

Homework Assignment

I am asking you for your own good, while you are wallowing in self-pity about your house, to stop for a moment and make out your own list of blessings that God has bestowed on your life. I will even start you off; here are some of the things on my list.

For 44 years, 11 months, 6 days and counting, God has allowed me to wake up every morning, in my right mind, filling my lungs with breathe, while the sun fills my sight with golden rays of love. He has filled my world with love as I act as daughter, mother, sister, friend, granddaughter, mentor, author and sounding board—the list goes on and on daily.

God placed joy in my life, in the form of my children, whom I am pleased to guide through the pitfalls of this world, helping to direct them to the only one who can ever save them. Thank you Father for all the laughter that they have brought to my life, and when their laughter proved infectious, you increased it, adding even more joy to my cup, through my nieces and nephews—Allen, Christopher, Alina, Michaela, Mikey, Trent, Tori, and Lauren. Oh, I thank you Father for those blessings and the many more that are sure to come.

I'm sorry, I get a little caught up, but it is hard for me not to thank Him. Okay you can take it from there, how has God blessed you? Be sure and add as many pages as you need. If you are anything like me, you will probably need a whole notebook, but keep writing until you feel better. Praise your way to peace. How does this help you in the foreclosure? It is like a taking that spoon full of sugar, to help the rest of this medicine go down.

My Blessings

	Thank you, God for…
1.	

3

Nothing Happens By Chance

"May His will be done here on earth, as it is in heaven"
Matthew 6:10

Nothing ever happens by chance. So let us be sure that we understand the ultimate purpose of the foreclosure, by first looking at the definition.

Webster's Dictionary defines foreclosure as "to take away or the right to redeem". The mortgage company is tired of waiting for you to decide if you are going to work with them, and pay the note. They decided to "redeem", or take back your house.

Christ foreclosed on our souls, he died to redeem them or take them back. You can do the same, redeem, you can take back the property back by getting rid of the mortgage company.

God could have left things as they were, allowing us to die in our sins, we seem to enjoy sinning so much more than obeying anyway, but he just could not give up, and walk away without trying to save us from hell.

Are you just going to give up on your home, just walk away? God decided rather than give up he would work a plan that would redeem our souls.

True we are not God but we are in his image, and have power to cause change, and we too can redeem things if we choose to do so. Remember, when God did it, there was much planning and much work that lead up to the point in which Jesus could go down into hell and pay for our salvation. Actually, the Bible is an account of that plan, and shows the amount of effort necessary to enact that plan.

As a child of God, you will have to work just as hard, and have even more faith to redeem or save your house. Things will be happening around you that are not, what they appear to be. Everything that occurs is happening for your good if you trust the Lord.

Simply put, it may not be the intention of God that you lose your home, but he does honor your will. If you are demonstrating with your life, disobedience, using your house note for other bills, proving that you do not want the home, then you will have just that.

Review your past actions, and see just what they conclude. To do that we need to look into you as a person and see what the problem really is, and why you are standing here in jeopardy at this place in time.

Looking into your self can provide the insight needed to choose the path right for your foreclosure dilemma. It will cause you to either change something right now, or move on and come back to this same point again, later in life.

In this life, if you do not pass the course, you will have to repeat the class. Go through this lesson, without just throwing in the towel and giving up. There are obviously some changes needed, and now is the best time to do just that.

If you are throwing in the towel, then make sure that you made the adjustments, so that the towel lands in the right pile, thus ending favorably.

My mother reminds me everyday that in order to get different results you need to take a different course of action. Only you can cause change in your life, do something different. Find out why you are in financial cardiac arrest, and cause change. God has given you all the things needed to lead a prosperous life, but you have to do the work to make the harvest fruitful.

The abilities and talents endowed were provided to fulfill an undeniable purpose, in your life. The work involves spending the time with God to understand how you are to use that talent, fitting into the plan that serves others.

Every person has a purpose that serves others, the doctor helps to heal, the painter paints, and the pastor points to salvation. Understanding just what role each person is supposed to fulfill, or determining how they are to serve is a difficult task, that takes commitment to God, and his Word.

Have you tapped into your purpose? I personally have wasted a lot of my life running around doing a little here, doing a little there, living a famine or feast lifestyle. I was trying to live my will, going through life my way.

I didn't know any better, no strike that, I did know, but I chose to make up my own purpose, rather than seek God's Will for my life. I skated all around the tasks that God intended for me, making excuses, when I could have attended to my father's business. I probably would have still been skating had my own foreclosure not made me stop and face my own mirror.

One day after much prayer, I was lead to read Deuteronomy 28:1-10. After reading the passages, I suddenly understood that obedience is the most vital piece of a prosperous life, and the only way to follow the narrow path. Obedience, would lead to the place prepared for me, where foreclosure was no longer a part of my life. I had been lost and I did not even realize it.

I developed faith, through various tests, but that was still not enough. I was not obedient. I was picking and choosing which of God's laws I would follow. I thought it was nothing wrong with hanging out with the folks, smoking and drinking.

I did not understand that my relationship with God was not strong enough to combat their relationship with the world. When my friends would say things that I knew were contrary to God's path, I would go along because it felt good.

I had to understand that those feelings of wanting to fit in, and feeling good, were merely distractions ultimately serving to interrupt my signal from God. Without a clear signal, I would hear only what I wanted to hear, not what God was trying to tell me. My connection to God was like a bad cell signal, full of static, except it was God on the other end, and I could only get small bits of his messages. That bad signal allowed me to miss the important things that God needed to tell and show me, things that would have served to help me avoid traps, and pitfalls like foreclosure. Without that clear signal, I was defenseless, and subject to unnecessary plight.

I had to seek a clear signal, and the only way to get that was through the word. I had to spend more time with God, seeking his purpose for my life.

My well had run dry, and this time I did not know where to dig to replace it. In the past, I might have hustled up a way to temporally, digging a fresh well, to make my situation better, but this time all my efforts failed. It was as if God was putting his foot down, and demanding that I no longer try my useless methods, but firmly place my foot on his path. He was demanding that his Will be mine, and I could accept that or not. Save my house or loss it.

You do know, that His' plan is not always your plan, don't you? My plan, my will was not in line with God's plan, and so this time in order to get what I wanted, my house, he availed no other option than to follow His plan.

I had to get rid of all the distractions, and stop allowing interruptions to his signal. All the things I enjoyed doing like hanging out, going out for drinks at the bar, waiting to meet a man by chance, all had to go. Kicking it at the clubs so late on Saturday night, that getting up for church on Sunday was impossible, had to stop.

God's plan was so much better than mine. When I got rid of the distractions, it was just as if, a huge veil was lifted, revealing the truths that I had not seen until now. I knew what I needed to do to save my home, and I had the faith to go and do it.

This is what worked in my life, propelling me to hear, and walk with God a few times everyday. Each person will have a different change for their life when they look into the mirror.

What worked for me, may not work for you. Your problem might be controlling your spending down at the Casino, it is just entertainment, not a job, and I hope you know that.

Someone else might just need to stop smoking weed, buying two $20 bags a day, and then at the end of the month wondering why you cannot pay your house note.

Maybe you did not learn how to properly use your charge cards, spending too much of your paycheck on outfits, that you cannot even wear.

Your foreclosure is a symptom of a deeper problem, just like a headache, or a soar throat. Not having the money to pay your mortgage is not the real problem. You must identify the root of your problem, and create a plan caused change.

You cannot just look at my solution and apply it to your situation, you will need to look in your own mirror and start there.

What may appear to be a proven solution for one person, in fact may be an unattainable path for another. I mention this now because many times, I have worked with people, and we thought that we had the right path in trying to save their home, but all the options were blocked.

There was one woman who I tried to help, who had been away for an extended period, out of the country, and left her home, and the house-note for her sister to pay, on her behalf.

After two years, she returned and found that the sister had let the house go into foreclosure. While she was away, she had developed a relationship with a married man. He had moved out of the house of his wife and children, and now planned to move in with her. When the two of them decided to try to save the foreclosed house where they were planning to live together, every option was blocked.

They needed to look at the person in the mirror and ask the question, "What is the real reason I am here". Maybe God's plan did not entail making it easy for that man to leave his family. Maybe adultery is one of those laws God is particular about. Maybe this disobedience would lead to a much worst state of affairs, excuse my pun.

It reminded me of a story in the bible about a man riding a donkey down a road on which the Lord sent an angel to block his path. Every time the man urged his donkey to move forward on the path, the donkey stopped, as he could not get past the angel who blocked the way with a flaming sword. The donkey could see the angel, but the man could not. The donkey, seeing the angel, would not move, and, if he had, the angel would have killed him and his rider.

Nothing can change until you adjust the formula for your life, and address your specific issues. Maybe you should look at the person in your mirror.

In the case of the woman returning from living abroad, and residing with her leave-in boyfriend, who was still married, the changes needed were screaming. They, of course, refused to acknowledge change. In time and she wound up losing her home, and moving in with her mom. I bet he didn't move in there. He probably took his butt back home, where he should have been from the start.

I know that someone else may look at this whole foreclosure thing and say, "Well, had you just paid your house note like every body else, you wouldn't be in this trouble." What happens, if you have paid it on time for years, and suddenly the well that provided the mortgage payment dries up?

That is exactly what happened to me, the well dried up and suddenly I was once again, faced with finding a new resource, to pay my mortgage.

I mean in life do "wells" just dry up, leaving you with the chore of locating a new source for water? You had better believe it is real, but remember each source of distress is different, and my problems are only because of my disobedience, with regard to not fulfilling my purpose.

My well, was only temporary, and I was supposed to move on to a new well long ago. In reflection, I came across a story in 1Kings 2:8. The Lord directed Elijah to various places telling him to go here, drink here, and when the river dried up go the next place. God was telling Elijah step-by-step just where to go, and how long to stay in that place.

What would have happened had Elijah not been obedient? What if Elijah had gone on to places that God had not prepared for him to go? He would have suffered as others, losing ground, as they lost the provisions of God. Are you suffering from working your own will?

Maybe you are too comfortable sitting in your boat; selling your illegal DVD's. Couldn't you see it was time to find a legal hustle? O.K. now you are out your of the boat. Now is your time to do that thing, to fulfill purpose, seeking your path.

I did not act on what was really my responsibility, my purpose, until I too was kicked out of my boat. Thank God, I realized before a whale swallowed me up.

The next time that I was kicked out of my boat, I did what I needed to do in enough time to save my home, but I pay off. I would not have felt committed to follow the path if I had not looked inside of me--praying that God would lead me to the answer.

"The punishment that you gave me was the best thing that could have happened to me, for it taught me to pay attention to your laws." Psalms 119:71-72.

When you get tired of trying to force things, your "will", your way, try His way. Consult the Lord,

He will direct you to a path far better than anything you could ever have dreamed or imagined.

We must be aware of the paths that we must take, and those that we must avoid. As a child of God, we have an internal meter that helps us to discern or sort out the right from the wrong path. We must first take the time to clear our minds, so that we have a clear signal, and can pay attention and obediently allow His will, to rule over our lives. We are instructed to pray in every situation, during good times and bad, giving thanks to God, for "nothing" happens by chance, not even your foreclosure.

4

Faith or Fear

"And the very hairs of your head are all numbered. So don't worry" Matthew 10:30-31

Often when people finally come to my office seeking a workable solution, they tell me that, when they first received their foreclosure notice, all they could think to do was pray, and that is good.

They said, "They were afraid of losing their homes, and guess what?" Their fears became reality. They allowed it to be so, by not moving in a positive direction, putting themselves in a position to receive, and why...because fear froze them.

That is how fear works, it tricks you by freezing you from doing things that you would normally do in order to avoid a situation. Think about the horror movies. The one who is so afraid of being caught, who can't do anything but stand there and scream, usually is the one caught.

I understand that foreclosure is a scary thing (been there, done that), but one has to do more than stand there and scream. It is still a process, and we must understand that we can affect that process. Foreclosure can be stopped, it can be slowed down, it can be changed, and it can be avoided.

Your faith in God and walking in the light of that faith will allow you to avoid the thing you fear, but fear will not allow you to do any of those things, so long as you allow it to control you. You must pray past the fear, as faith is the only weapon that effectively works. Fear and faith are opposites, and so it is impossible to have both, true faith and fear at the same time. Fear is actually faith in reverse.

So when the people who finally come to the office seeking help, and are no longer so afraid that they can't move, and have also gotten pass the other enemy called embarrassment, they can begin to change or resolve the situation.

Embarrassment is a cousin to pride and, therefore, serves the same purpose of stopping you in your tracks. I have had so many people tell me that they were too embarrassed to ask for help, and then it was so late. They tried the way of the ostrich, burying their heads in the ground, hoping that it would just go away. Many times these are the same people who move without asking any questions. They receive the first letter in the mail, not fully reading the mortgage company's attempt for communication, only catching sight of the word "foreclosure" or "sheriff's sale" and then they move.

These people are giving up before they have finished the race. They did not give God a chance to help them. Sure, they prayed but it was like empty words, because there was no faith, no commitment behind the words. Therefore, without true faith, there surely was no way to keep their home. I guess you are thinking that if the mortgage company mentions the word "foreclosure", time is up, but that is not the reality. Let me tell you about a real life situation.

A woman decided that she just was not going to fight, but merely move from her home of 35 years. She only owed a balance of $10,000.00 on a house that is worth $65,000.00. By the time she finally decided to come into my office, she had moved most of her things out of the house, in an attempt to abandon the property. She had seen my ad in the newspaper, and she suddenly wondered if there was something more that she could do while she moved her things. I asked her to bring in with her any documentation that she had received recently from her mortgage company.

She brought in 5 envelopes of which only one had been opened. When I read her documents, the mortgage company was asking if she would consent to refinancing the balance owed to avoid foreclosure. All that she had read was the word "foreclosure," and assumed that she was out of time.

She had missed only two payments, and that was due to her being in the hospital with a broken hip. As you can see, fully reading all the letters on the page is a vital defense in avoiding foreclosure. Don't be a fool for fear, and certainly don't let fear fool you.

As I mentioned, she had already moved from the property, and wanted to know if she could just get rid of the house through a quick sell, while she still owned it. She had decided that a nursing home offered a better environment for her in her declining years. We helped her to find a buyer who bought the house for $40,000.00, giving the buyer $20,000.00 in equity, and the old lady, walked away with $30,000.00 in cash, after she satisfied the outstanding mortgage.

Let me slow down and explain. The equity is the difference between what the house is worth, minus any outstanding loans. In this scenario, the balance she owed was $10,000.00 and the house was worth $65,000.00. Therefore, she had $55,000.00 in equity.

When she sold the house for $40,000.00 of which she owed an original mortgage of $10,000.00, and after paying the buyers closing cost, which totaled, $2,500.00 left her a $27,500.00 profit. The house was worth $65,000.00 so when the new owner paid $40,000.00 for the house, that left him $20,000.00 in equity.

House worth	$65,000.00
Mortgage Balance	$10,000.00
Equity	$55,000.00
Property sales for	$40,000.00
Closing costs	-$2500.00
Pay Off Mortgage	-$10,000.00
Seller Nets	$27,500.00
*Buyer's Equity	$20,000.00

*Equity is not cash, but can be accessed via equity line with the bank.

This is a win-win scenario. She got rid of her foreclosure by paying off the debt, and walking away with cash to start anew. This is something that anyone can do, whether the sheriff sale has occurred or not, as long as you understand how to use your rights.

This is an effective use of "redemption". You need to check your state to understand the redemption rights for your area, as each state establishes its own rights for redemption. Redemption is the right that determines how much time you will have to "take back" your property after the sheriff sale has occurred.

In some states, the time may be as long as 12 full months, in other places it may only be 30 days, while in other states there is no redemption period at all. It is important, while you are structuring your foreclosure options, to understand your rights as is applies to your particular state.

You can go to your county web site and review the foreclosure procedures, which will discuss just how long you have to redeem your property. You are trying to create a plan, and in order for it to be workable, you must do the necessary research.

The more time you have the more options you will discover, so why not stop here, and go and research your redemption process for foreclosure in your state.

In Michigan, the period is 6 months, Georgia only 30 days, yet as I mentioned earlier some states do not offer this grace period at all, while other states have a period of almost a year. Task two is to understand the parameters of the redemption law for the state, in which your property is situated.

As I stated at the beginning you need to do your own research, so that you can understand the redemption procedures for your state. There is a website you should check out, which provides a great overview by *RealtyTrac*.com.

RealtyTrac maintains statistics for the real estate industry, and therefore has a detailed presentation of the foreclosure process for every state.

The headings include, judicial and non-judicial which refer to the process that must be taken in order to start a foreclosure. In judicial, the lender files the appropriate court action against the owner in default. Usually this is in the form of a pending lawsuit against the owner. If it rules against the owner, the court will order a public sale of the property.

I urge you to visit the RealtyTrac web site for more detail. For our purposes, we will look at the process period--the length of time prior to the actual sale of the property, and the sale publication--length of time that must be publicized, prior to the sale of the property.

These items spell time to you and, regardless where you are in this process, if your property did not go to the sheriff's sale, you still can work out an arrangement that will allow you to resume paying your mortgage. Finally, the redemption period allows you a final attempt to purchase back your house by paying the full amount of the foreclosure price.

This can be done, via cash, refinance, or you can arrange for an investor, to buy the house on your behalf. Should you select this method, you would then lease your property from that investor for 24 or 48 months, and then refinance the house back into your own name, as you should be able to obtain a mortgage at that time.

You want to be sure that your lease payments are going directly to the new mortgage payments, so you will need to take some additional steps to protect your ownership in the property using this method.

Be sure and talk to an attorney so that she can create a document to protect your remaining interest in the property.

5

Communication Is Key

"Then they cried out to the Lord in their troubles, and
He helped them and delivered them"
Psalms 107:19

It is important for you to understand exactly what the foreclosure means, and how it can affect you now and in the future. So let's be sure that we understand just what the foreclosure means.

Foreclosure is the process by which the mortgage company takes back your portion of the house that you bought with them. I am at this point referring to foreclosures with a mortgage company, but please be aware that they are not the only ones who can foreclosure on your property.

Your house and your mortgage are two separate things. When you bought your home, what you really did was offer the mortgage company the opportunity to invest with you as an equal partner in the ownership of this house. You have a relationship with your mortgage company. One that does not require you to call them unless there is trouble, and then they want to work with you to solve the problem.

The mortgage company puts up the cash for you to buy the house and, in return, they expect that you would not only pay the money back a little bit at a time, but you would also maintain the property, taxes, and insurance. Your support on these issues helps both in the relationship to protect the investment.

Oddly, the relationship between you and the mortgage company has other partners, who also have the right to foreclose. The other partners in the investment of this new mortgage consist of the county, which assesses property tax, and the insurance company providing a homeowner's policy.

Your mortgage company is not the only entity with the ability to foreclose. If you don't pay the property taxes on the house, the county can decide to auction it off as well. Each year counties across the nation auction off many houses whose taxes remain unpaid for two consecutive years, but this too can be avoided, by simply communicating.

In the event that the county decides to foreclose, they will essentially ask you and your partner the mortgage company, to pay the taxes current, or they will sale the property to get the money. One way or another, the county will get their tax monies.

As you see, the relationship you have with your mortgage company is very important. If they decide that you are simply not holding up your end of the bargain, making your payments or communicating the intention of making the payments, then they have no choice but to end the relationship and foreclose on the property.

It is much like a pending divorce, which is what they are trying do. Let's say that you are sick of your husband, and he just won't do any of the things he agreed to do when you got married. Worse yet he won't even talk to you about it, giving you some kind of indication that he intends to do better.

You threaten him and he still does not respond, so you contact your attorney to file divorce papers hoping that he sees that you are serious and you will make a last ditch effort to fix the relationship. That is all your foreclosure is and, just like the saving of a marriage, you can convince the mortgage company to stop the proceedings, and get back to keeping up your end of the marriage.

The mortgage company does not want your house, they simply want your payment or some form of communication notifying your intentions. They are not in the real estate business and consider it a burden to sell the property. They would prefer your communicating with them and thereby working together to find a workable solution to the problem of your inability to keep your end of the bargain.

Communicating in a relationship seems to keep popping up, doesn't it? Talking to God, communicating with the mortgage company, that sounds like there could be some sort of connection.

Letting people know what is going on, is the best way to keep stress off, of you, as it leads the way to finding or creating workable solutions. Not only in your prayer life, but in all relationships you must open your mouth and speak from your heart.

Clients approaching foreclosure often ask me, "What do I say to the mortgage company?" My response is always the same. Tell them the truth. You intend to keep your house, you suffered a financial setback, and now you are in a new place, or whatever the story may be, tell them the truth.

The mortgage company is not the only one listening. You can also tell your family and friends. The bottom-line is that you not lose the investment of your home. It is critical, and you are doing all the other things, as you should, then maybe you must begin to ask those around you for help.

Tell them the truth; you need help to keep your home. Ask as many people as you can, ask them all to give you a little, and soon it will be more than enough.

One woman that called had done just that. She contacted every person she knew and asked them for help. Some people gave her $50 or $100 but soon she had the money to give to the mortgage company, and her friends didn't want her to even try to pay them back, because they were just happy to help. Tell people what is going on. Ask for help, open your mouth after all, you are only human. Who knows, they may one day need your help as well.

I used to tell my husband all the time that he should be open and honest with people. He would reply, that you should not tell people any more than what they ask, and I disagree.

At our wedding reception my father's favorite cousin, to whom my father he had bragged to for months, telling him about his "big time engineer" son-in-law, who was working at Cadillac Motor. He approached my husband and with a big grin stuck out his hand and said, "So you're the big time engineer". My husband looked at this man squarely in the face and gave him a dry, flat "No". The man stood there with his mouth open, the smile had disappeared, and now his face looked like one big question mark.

He repeated his question to my husband again, "you are an engineer, right". To which my husband nodded "yes". The man just walked away, and started talking to someone else. My husband, not sure why the man walked away, turned to me and said, "Well what's wrong with him".

I explained, the man was trying to communicate with you, and was expressing his pride in the fact that his cousin, my father, was so proud to have an engineer as a son-in-law. You burst his bubble with your smugness, and further you blocked his attempts to communicate with you by not offering a suitable rebuttal.

I realize this story was a little off the subject, but the point is "talk". When you are trying to communicate with the mortgage company, tell them the truth. They are listening. They just want a reasonable explanation and solution for the delinquency of your mortgage payments. Tell them your story, tell them what is going on, bear your soul, and they are more likely to offer a workable solution.

They do not want your house. They want to find a reason to allow you to keep it. These days many of the banks and mortgage companies have developed all new programs to help people, as they read and see the news as well. They know that times are hard and, guess what, if they backed out of all of the relationships in which people were in financial turmoil, they too would soon be trying to talk someone into allowing them to keep their home as well.

So help them, to help you. Talk to the bank, before they feel forced to send your house, to the sheriff sale. Give them a reason to help you. Make some payment arrangements that you can afford. Do not just agree to the first thing they offer you; tell them what you honestly can afford. This will eliminate problems down the road with broken payment arraignments.

Assignment 3

Track your communication with the mortgage company.

Do not stick your head in the sand expecting it to all just go away. Let's give them a call right now. Keep notes below of your conversation, they can only say "no". Below is the information you need to keep track of, so make your notes.

What is date of the conversation? _________
Who did you talk to? __________________
What did you agree?

____

____

____

____

____

When are you to do it?

____

____

____

When is the next time you are to communicate?

____

6

Seek Purpose

"The punishment you gave me was the best thing...for it taught me understanding" Psalm 119:71-72

In seeking purpose for my life, through truth, armed with the knowledge that there is nothing, that I could ever do, to stop God from loving me, I found understanding of many more things than just foreclosure. Now I understood that there were times in my life when I was in perfect line with His will, doing as I was supposed to do. Then there were others when stepped off the path, without even realizing it.

You can always tell when you are in line with His will, things just sort of fall in place, and it will even seem that all of nature will be smiling at you. I can remember one specific time when I was in line, on the path doing as God intended for my life, the day I married my husband.

I had prayed many times in the months and weeks before our wedding, to be sure that it was he, that I was supposed to marry. Each time, the answer confirmed that he was the one.

We were married in Detroit, Michigan in the fall when the air is generally so cold and crisp, turning the leaves on the trees the deepest shades of gold, and burgundy. Not this day, our day the temperature was 81 degrees and sunny. The sky was blue, and the birds were singing as I sat in the limousine 20 minutes before the wedding, praying that I was in line with His word.

I felt this kind of peace only a couple of other times in my life since. I knew truly, that I was doing what I was supposed to do.

Some of the other times that I can remember are when I gave birth to my children, provided shelter for the homeless, and when I started writing books for the good of others.

Knowing your purpose and completing it as God requires, will fill you with peace. The hard part is staying on the path, or more realistically knowing when you have stepped off, and understanding how to get back quickly.

In the case of my marriage, we were happy for many years, and blessed beyond my wildest dreams. That's what happens, when you follow God's path, you just know it. I never knew how happy marriage could have made me, and I was content for a long while.

Then the path turned and we didn't. I say that we didn't, because I was a part of my husband, and although I was honoring our vows, and he wasn't, I was still a part of him.

I felt that we had been tricked, into following the suggestions of evil, and I allowed that force to lead us away from our path. By the time the smoke cleared, we were literally standing on two different paths, as we had lost our way, our home, and our marriage.

Looking back, we were lucky, as we could have lost, a lot more than that. There are people sitting in jail right now who lost those same things and without God, lost their minds allowing their emotions to lead them down unimaginable paths, but that is another story.

Mental note: be careful of the whispers in your ear. They are not always in line with God's Will. Your associates may think that they are helping you by giving their advice, but if they too are still lost, then they can hardly be the ones to lead you out of the dark. If they are not in line with God, then where do you think their advice will lead you?

No other way to turn. My children and I returned to God's path. Through the tears, and fears, I still only had the love of God to sustain me. It's easy for me to say that now, but when I went through foreclosure and divorce all at the same time, boy was it hard to say and believe. Yes, we lost our house, but I knew that God would provide for me on the other side, if I continued to trust, and obey, and boy did he ever!

Many times when these struggles manifest, they offer two options--lose your mind doing things you normally would not do, or trust God and scurry back to the path that He has laid before you. Just ask yourself—"Am I really on a path that will give honor to God?" Will my actions benefit someone other than myself?

I am a good talker, and one who loves people--all people, so much so, that I will try to have a conversation with any person. If I am standing in line at the grocery store or in the bank, I always am able to strike up a conversation with the people around me. Is this a blessing or a curse?

When I told you that I felt I sometimes changed into the people, that I hung around, I was talking specifically about my past business partners. As I talked to people getting into their heads, over time they got into mine.

I allowed them to change my thinking. If it was someone who was nice and they were adulterers, then somehow I would start thinking along their lines. Their whispers became my actions, even though I knew better, and hated the things that they were doing.

Years before my financial distress, I had a business that helped people to obtain small business loans. This venture I undertook with a zealous partner. My partner was in charge of bringing new clients, and I was always amazed at the number of people that he was bringing through the doors. He too was a great talker. He was much like me, talking to everyone, but he was charming people out of their life savings, I later learned. When I found that he was promising them things that we could not provide and then collecting fees for it, I cut my ties with him.

Then I had the responsibility to find clients to keep my office open, and I soon found that I was doing the very same things that he had done. I too found myself promising things that were impossible to deliver. I had turned into what I hated.

Clearly I was not using my talents to serve God, only myself. I had the talent to communicate with anyone, even perfect strangers. Instead of finding ways to be a blessing to them, I allowed myself to be a curse.

If you want to know if you are on God's path, ask yourself an important question. "Am I using my talents in a purpose that is pleasing to God, Am I providing for others?" Once I realized that I was out of line, I had to change my way of thinking, before the Lord forced a change upon me. I suggest that you do the same. Remember there is a purpose in everything. Nothing happens by chance.

I realize that you picked up my book to understand foreclosure, and find the means to fight it. What you do not understand is that you must cause change to make your life different.

Please bear with me, and hear the message and ignore the messenger. After all this is my path, easing you through this difficult time in your life. What better ointment shall I use than the truth?

Foreclosure for me was a bitter lesson, yes. While it served as a "gut check", it forced me to create understanding that allows help for others. In the hard light of reality, it really served to be a window, opened by God, taking me, and my children to a better life.

Of all the things I have come to understand, the most important foundation is the manner with which I interface. My interfacing with God and my neighbors must be out of love. This has nothing to do with how often I go to church, or how many times I serve as an usher. It is however, my day-to-day, minute-by-minute, relationship with God, that directs my life. It is the most important premise and actually holds the seed of prosperity in every aspect of life, and may be part of the reason you are in foreclosure.

I understand the meaning of prosperity. I now know that prosperity is beyond money, but actually encompasses wholeness. I have come to understand, that prosperity means "nothing missing". Listening to voices of truth including Creflo Dollar, and Wilma Johnson, whose messages have helped me to focus and understand what true prosperity really means.

I mention Dr. Dollar's interpretations because many people misunderstand him, because they cannot get past his name, and so are not listening to the message he is trying to convey. I have heard many people say that he is all about money. I wonder if his name were Melvin Blank would they feel the same, would they bother to listen to the lessons, then?

People should listen to the message and block out the messenger. If you have never listened to Creflo Dollar, you truly owe it to yourself. I want you to read an important section that provides a foundation for critical insight into the very basis of Dr. Dollar's teachings, and bears repeating now, as we build hope in your current circumstances.

Check out Deuteronomy 28:11, and read for yourself just what God wants to bless us with, prosperity. "The LORD will grant you abundant prosperity—in the fruit of your womb, the young of your livestock and the crops of your ground—in the land He swore to your forefathers to give you".

I think that it demonstrates God's grace all the more articulately when the person pointing out a path, appears to be standing on it at the same time.

If the pastor directing me to prosperity is standing in obvious lack, what am I to think, or believe. I think that many people cannot come out of the world, out of the dark, because they can't see the difference.

If they see you are still struggling, cursing and crying your way through day after day, putting on a "fake face", what then will compel them to want to change their life?

However, if they see you are prosperous, happy, full of joy even in the midst of madness, they will be compelled to want to understand why, and may start their relationship with God to see how they can come up to that same point.

Being filled with "God's peace" simply is something you cannot fake. When you are truly, a child of light, people will see it in you, and want the light to shine through them as well. When you go through struggles, and yes, you will have moments of tears, but the faith inside you will count it all joy.

The goal of every Christian should be wholeness, which can only come from reading and studying the word. If I want to be whole, or prosperous, then I lack nothing in my heart, my home, my health, and my finances. To achieve this state of peace, which is not available in any store; one must begin to grow it in their heart.

Changing your life is the only way to get off the treadmill of "just getting by", and then you can tap into your power to make your life different. You want to save your house, and avoid foreclosure, then seek the purpose for your life, and turn to the obedience of loving God.

When I first began to study The Word, I understood that all I needed to do is *"ask and it would be given"* (Matthew 7:7). I tried asking in the same manner as many baby Christians, asking in prayer, all the things that I thought I should have.

I sat around, wishing, as if God was a big Sears's catalog, that I had things that were of no purpose. Then when the things I asked for did not materialize, or I did not receive what I asked for, I got upset with God.

Yes, I too was like so many other baby Christians, who first begin learning about God, asking for various things over, and over again, then sitting back waiting for the UPS man to show up with all my blessings wrapped up with a giant bow on top.

I was quite upset when I did not receive my cherry red, drop top Porsche, so what if I hadn't worked to gain it. So what that I had sent up a blank prayer, I simply assumed that the Lord had said "No" to my prayer, and so I just wished for something else.

I mention this because many of the people in foreclosure do the very same thing. They wish for God to save their home, but they take no responsibility in placing themselves in a position to receive the blessing. There is no effort, no belief, and therefore no fruition. "Oh, save my house God", they cry into our pillows every night and then all day long, watching reruns of "One Life to Live", and "Judge Judy", while waiting for God to deliver.

We do that because many simply don't know any better. We treat God the same way we treat the rest of our lives, lazy and half-hearted. Doing only the basic requirements, minimally giving effort to activities, our jobs, prayers, and our families, doing just enough to get by. We don't dive into our jobs, our careers, or the Word therefore, we get out no more than what we put in.

We must learn to plant seeds. We plant seeds by taking steps in a positive direction placing ourselves in a position to receive God's blessings. We must trust God enough to seek and find a method, create a plan and work it until He tells you to do something different.

It is an insult to God when He has so much for us, and we are content with just enough. We pray and God makes provisions to answer those prayers based on our ability to trust and follow His directions; working toward the position to receive the blessing. We just scratch the surface, talking a good game about trusting in the Lord, all the while seeking ways around the work required to receive the blessing.

I, myself, had been guilty many times in my life, which accounts for my famine or feast lifestyle. In retrospect, had it not been for that "famine or feast" way of life, my shortcomings, I would not be here in this place writing words in hope of encouraging someone else.

When I worked at growing in the Word, I learned that it is not always the evil forces blocking me from God blessings, but many times, it was just me, and my disobedience blocking those blessings. Not trusting in the Lord, to get up, and go out, and do what I knew that I ought to be doing.

The only way for me to understand what I was supposed to do, and where I was supposed to go was to search the Word, digging into my bag of seed. The bag of seed is the Bible, and to plant the crop that I needed to grow, meant studying and focusing nightly, burying the seeds in my heart. It meant reading the same text over, and over again, until it spoke to me. It meant opening my eyes and ears to the things around me, as God used people to get messages and directions to me, His child.

It meant diligently working, to gain understanding of the Word, and then applying the things I learned in my daily tasks, as well as loving God, loving my family, as well as all my neighbors. I must accomplish my task as a "Child of God" with honor, giving all that I can in everything I do, if I want to be prosperous.

As a "Child of God", surviving is not good enough. I must be prosperous so that I can be the head, and not the tail, be the giver and not the borrower, with my cup over flowing having much to give away for the honor and glory of my Father's name. This glory to God causes others to want to do the same, and serves to help them find their way out of the darkness.

This way of life holds no room for me to be jealous of another person, but being happy where God placed me. Many of us spend our time wishing we were someone else, thinking that someone else's life looks so much better than that of our own. That energy could be used to seeking out your own purpose.

I love Mary J Blige, I can feel God's love through many of the songs she sings, but I would not want to be her or Lauren Hill, or Beyonce, Janet, Queen Latifa, J Lo, or India Aire. These beautiful talented sisters are who they are, because they are following paths set aside for them.

God established our paths before any of us were born. They have simply taken the initiative to realize their purpose, and through their actions are serving to soothe life through sound and art. How many other "would be", "supposed to be", singers, writers, doctors, lawyers, preachers, teachers, are sitting back in a "life foreclosure" wondering what the heck, they are doing wrong? The "would be" Sara Lee's, Kim Worthy's, Michael Jordan's, Cuba Gooding's, or Barack Obama's sitting back willing to continue taking life on the chin rather than seeking their true purpose, and realizing the abundance God has set aside just for them.

God has blessings set aside just for you, and only you. My blessing is only for me. It may benefit you, but it is my path for me to walk. I remember reading somewhere that when we are jealous of others, we insult God, because we are not happy in where he has placed us.

I had to be happy and that meant I needed to work. I could not be weak, giving half of anything, but strong, giving 110% in all that I did. I would not only survive, but would be prosperous, able to engage my own Sears wish list, save my house, see the world, attain my heart's desires, because I first gave honor and glory to God.

Now that I am a mature "Child of God", I have a better understanding. I know God's system, ask for what I want, knowing that it will be granted, so long as I have the faith in God, and trust Him completely. So what is the difference?

Before understanding, I thought that merely asking was enough to make it so. I understand now, that trusting God means actively moving toward the request, in the knowledge that it will be fulfilled.

Now, instead of sitting around asking God to save my house, I had to get up and go out, secure in the fact that my prayer would be answered, as long as I did my part, which started as soon as I said Amen. That also meant remembering that God works through relationships, and, again, I had to be in the right place seeking the right relationship in order to allow the manifestation of the blessing.

If saving my house meant that I needed to have a better paying job, then it was up to me. It was my responsibility of earnestly working toward attaining that goal. Maybe it would mean working two crappy jobs, until one great job availed itself, but certainly did not mean that I just sat around and waited for a job to come along.

"Seek God first" is the very best way to describe this new way to achieve the otherwise unattainable. I pray asking God to place me, and then I actively go out and do all that I can to be in the position to receive the job. In the words of Creflo, "if my problem is not having a job, then looking for a job, is my job."

I didn't lose my house, because I worked to save it. I got up off my knees asking God to make a way, and looked for and actively sought the windows that He provided, not afraid to go through, because I had blessed assurance that He was with me, making my way to attain the goal, out of no where. I put myself in a position to receive God's blessings. I contacted the mortgage company pleaded my case as many times as necessary with confirmed humility, until I received a workable answer.

Faith in God does not ensure that we understand His way, but we close our eyes and follow the sound of His voice leading us beside the still waters. What is the sound of His voice? It is the Holy Spirit that has been put inside His children as a guide, but without studying His Word you will never be able to hear.

So I ask you, the client, what is your relationship with God? Your relationship with God and your ability to apply active prayer, followed by effort driven faith, will help you to understand the promptings from the Holy Spirit.

I am not a preacher, nor a teacher, but merely a Child of God who has been on many journeys through many storms, and in deserts throughout my own life. I have also had the pleasure of experiencing extreme blessings in my life, while also living vicariously through the lives of others.

Equally, God has corrected me many times, as I walked on the wrong path, and have repeated many lessons that were vital to my growth and own development.

7

Results of the Blessings

"For the earth and every good thing in it belongs to the Lord and is yours to enjoy"
1 Corinthians 11 10:26

So when we look at your house and it being in foreclosure we, must understand that the loss of that material item does not necessarily mean the lose of your blessing, but rather an opportunity for you to be in a position to receive new blessings and a brand new house.

In life, we sometimes become too content with our surroundings that we become deafened to the voice of God, directing us to do other things. We get the big promotion, then house and car, and we think that we have arrived. Yet there is so much more that needs to be done, all around us.

We forget that God has placed us in a better position, so that we can be of help or be a blessing to others. We are now “all that and a bag of chips”, and so we ignore the promptings of God.

God sits there and waits for us to remember it was only Him, who brought us out of our mess, and yet we don’t. He begins to tap us on the shoulder, to remind us.

I remember a sermon that could have been called, “But, God”. The messenger reflected on the bad things that had happened in his life, and how God could have left him, in his mess, but did not. God showed up and showed out. I cannot remember word for word, but I will put in my own words. God saw me making deals with the wrong kind of people, digging myself in more and more debt, and could have left me to the mercy of my creditors, *but God* stepped in, choose to pull me out.

God saw that the family who had worked so hard rescuing others from the shelter, was now being evicted. He could have let them be forced, into a shelter as well, *but God* made a way for us to move into a brand new house, and work on our credit, and finally buy a house that I could not have dreamed of.

My point is simple. He will intervene if you allow Him, and you allow Him by creating a relationship with Him. Now if you do not enter into a relationship, He will tap you on the shoulder until He finally gets your attention. A tap on the shoulder from God, is like being tapped by your mom, when you're making a bunch of noise in the church. At first, it is a tap touch indicating you are too loud, please be good. Then she taps you a bit harder, so that you turn around and see what it is you are doing wrong.

God will do whatever is necessary to get our attention. Look at Jonah, God kept tapping him on the shoulder to get him to heed to His command. That's what the great storm was all about.

The sailors on the boat were thrown around, because of one man trying to duck his assignment from God. They had no choice but to throw him overboard where God allowed a whale to swallow him, rather than drown. Finally, as he sat there reflecting on his blessings from God, he decided to obey, and heed the commands.

God tapping you on the shoulder will always be subtle at first, just small things, you losing your keys, lose your job, and lose your family, each time the taps get louder and louder. You may be in an accident, or worst you lose your home. Is your foreclosure a means for God to get your attention?

So many people come to my office and they say, "No, I go to church every Sunday, so God could not be trying to get my attention." My reply, I will state here because there are certain things some people just can't hear and, therefore, you don't say them to their face. You never know how someone will just snap and go nuts, so I hold my tongue many times, even when I do know the answer.

Just because you are in the church one or two hours every 7 days, does not make a relationship with God. It simply means that you are once again giving the minimal commitment, or only 30% if that, when you could do a lot more. Let me put it in a different way.

Let's say that you are dating, and you really, and truly love the person you are dating, but you can only see that person, two hours a day, once a week, or sometimes once every two weeks, or worst every two months. There is nothing keeping you from seeing that person more. Actually, you could see that person everyday, two or three times, but you choose to only talk to him when you are in trouble, or two hours once a week.

That would make a horrible relationship for me, as I love to be with the one I love. If God were like us then He too would spend the first 45 minutes of that occasional date complaining about the fact that you can only see each other 2 hours a week.

So my question is how much time are you investing in your relationship? I mean aside from church, when you go, are you kicking it with God? I once had a pastor who used to tell his congregation "you don't get a prize for just showing up". When you are in the church, is your mind there too, or is it already at the restaurant ordering your after service meal?

It is written, that where two are gathered in His name, He is present. But I wonder if many times we even know, that He is there. Give God all of you, and you may find you will have more pieces to go around.

God is love, and He created us to love Him, and you may find that "kicking it" with Him, spending time each day walking in His word to be a great thing. Many of us are careful to tithe our money, but what about ourselves. My pastor says that she proudly gives more than 10 percent in tithes. I bet she gives more than 10% of herself as well.

Let's, break that down, if I were to spend at least 10% of my time walking with God that would mean out of 24 hours in a day, 2 hours and 15 minutes belong to God.

Yes, that sounds ridiculous, but is it? I mean everyday if you are constantly talking to God, moment by moment, thanking Him as the blessings come your way, I think you can easily surpass that amount of time.

Every morning my granny reads the Word, with her breakfast. Many times her breakfast may last an hour or two. Then again, when she's in the car, and someone cuts her off in her lane, as she drives to the "Piggly Wiggly" and she is able to avoid an accident, she starts thanking God, right then and that may be another 2 or 3 minutes.

In the store, her can of peas is marked down 50 cents that gets another "Thank you God". She goes to the bank, talking to God as she goes, thanking Him for having something to put in, rather than having to take out. By the end of her day, when she sits down to read the Word again, she has spent far more than 10% of her day walking and talking with the Lord. Maybe that is what Solomon means when he refers to wisdom. It not something you can just pick up, it is a gift that must be sought. In my granny's 80 years, she has learned to do just that.

Many people don't start their walk with God, until a crisis, or hard tests come along, such as foreclosure or illness. Could be that God allows certain situations, so that people could come to themselves? Maybe getting them through the crisis will give them another tool with which they can help someone in that same situation. Could be that it is simply to induce a relationship that can last? Only God really knows, and you know what? I am glad.

So when the people in foreclosure claim that they have a good relationship with God, I encourage them, to really think about it. Most times, they come back and admit that maybe they have not been spending as much time with Him as they could. Therefore, they are not in a position of prosperity, and are lacking in crucial areas such as finances or organization.

I always remind them that I have been there myself. But trust, prayer, planning, organization, work, and persistence gave way to a new home that I am proud to say was a gift directly from God. After all, He does own all the houses on every hill.

In Psalms 50:11 God informs us clearly that; "*He owns all the cattle on a thousand hills*". Well guess what else sits on all those hills, His houses, so the loss of one amounts to nothing, because if you trust Him and remain faithful, He will give you another, fulfilling your wildest dreams, running your cup over beyond anything you could have ever dreamed or imagined.

8

Obedience the Path to Results

"If you will only let me help you, if you will only obey, then I will make you rich" Isaiah 3:19

God needs us to be obedient. If we are obedient, then He can use us to be a blessing to others. When I fell out of my boat, the convenience of simply accepting circumstances, "rolling with the punches", so to speak, my own home slipped into foreclosure. I soon realized that it was only because I allowed it to be. I was blocking God from using me, and therefore I was stuck in the trap of living in accordance with my will, and not His.

Yes, my own boat tipped over, landing me in water up to my neck. This was merely the result of my resistance to God who needed to use me as a tool. I was placed here, on this earth, at this time, for a specific purpose, and time was running out. I had come 44 years and still not started on my path.

In a way, I felt like I was Jonah, as the sea all at once seemed to knock my boat all around the ocean. My failure to obey was in fact disobedience to God, and He intended to use me, through words and actions to bless others. I refused to obey and do His will, so I was blocking my own blessings including the ability to pay my house note.

I realized all these things, and made a change in my life that allowed me to stand in the place to receive the blessing. I have told my clients, they must come to an understanding like this in their own life, and then do all that is possible, to positively bring forth the blessings. If the problem is not having the right job, find one you can do, even if you have to make a job up, start your own business, but find a way to stand in the place of the blessing.

What if Barry Gordy, ex-autoworker, had never started Motown? What if Patty blessed with talent never opened her mouth to sing? Many times obedience is stepping out on faith, with no more of a guarantee than to trust that God's path is so much better the one you are on now.

One of my favorite movies is Indiana Jones, "Search for the Holy Grail". In the movie, Harrison Ford has to follow clues in order to locate the mythical cup used to catch Christ's blood as he hung on the cross.

In the movie, Jones' dad had been shot and it was said that to drink from the cup, would heal his wound. So, Indiana read the clue which said *the man of God can trust Him, and will step out in faith.*

As he read the clue, he was standing at the mouth of a huge hole in the side of mountain. The ground was hundreds of feet below him, and to step out on faith would require someone who trusted God.

He took a deep breathe, closed his eyes and began to step, but hesitated, and pulled back his foot. He repeated the words, "Trust God", closed his eyes and took the important first step.

How often do we fail to take that all important first step? That goes back to what I told you earlier about planting a seed that God can bless. What Indy did not know was that there was a narrow path below him, invisible to the eye. So when he stepped out trusting God, He had already prepared the path allowing him to achieve his purpose. Remember that "is anything to hard for God?" (Genesis 18:14).

God is still in charge, and there is "no thing", no problem, no foreclosure that God cannot handle, for those who trust, in His grace. Trust means knowing that He will provide. So, live life like He already has answered your prayer, and thank Him in advance, continuing to move in a positive manner, making you receptive to the blessing.

Look at it this way, if your prayer was to become a doctor, you would need to do a lot more than just pray for it, wouldn't you? You would first pray that it was the path intended for you. The best way to answer that question is to understand that we all are supposed to serve each other here, below the sun.

In order for me to serve you the best, I should select something that I enjoy doing, and not just the job that will give me the biggest check. Your heart must be right to do that job. That way you will accomplish two tasks with the same action, pleasing God and loving your neighbor.

Some people were put here to sing sweet songs that bring peace to your heart, others are here to provide maintenance to that same heart through surgery, or exercise and therefore, still bring peace.

Be sure that you choose a job because of how it can be a benefit to someone else. In the word, God says that, "You didn't chose me, I choose you". Find out what he intends for you to do.

I remember in high school the nuns were trying to get us to understand which career we were best suited. They gave us an essay assignment with one question, "If you had $10 million, what would you do all day?"

If money really did not matter, what would we do all day? My answer was, sit on the beach and write books. What is your answer?

Next question is how do you get to that goal? You must work at whatever it is you are trying to do. If you ask any person who has achieved the purposes of their deepest desire, they will tell you that it took hard work, with many tests.

Face it, nothing comes easy, it is all a part of the test to see how badly you wish to achieve your goals. So once you've prayed, and you are sure that you have identified the position and the places, God can best use you in order to serve, you must act. You must be persistent in your need to accomplish the necessary tasks, whether it is going to school, practice speed sweeping, hitting 1000 golf balls a day or bouncing a basketball a million times a day, eventually you will achieve your goal.

Keep moving toward the goal, and when obstacles come and they will come, realize what they really are, move past them, and soon tests like foreclosure won't be able to affect you.

Nothing is easy, if it were, than anyone could do it. If I wanted to be a doctor, would I just pray that God make me a doctor, and then sit back and wait for my doctor's degree to come in the mail?

No, I would go to school, do an internship, and thereby put myself in a position to receive. Expect big things by starting with the completion of little ones.

9

Use Your Rights, Save Your Home

"Forgetting the past and looking forward to what lies ahead" Philippians 3:13

In the Bible, it states, *"that in all your getting, get understanding"*. You must understand your rights, including the foreclosure process. In each state, the process is different, and you need to understand exactly what you can expect.

When the bank finally decides that there is no other means for you to keep up your end of the bargain, pay your note, they will assign your mortgage to an attorney for foreclosure. They assign an attorney, to ensure that all rights are protected while the mortgage company exercises their right to sale the property.

In Michigan, the attorney will send you a letter informing you that the mortgage company intends to either accelerate the balance of your mortgage, unless you can make arraignments to ensure payment. To make clear this point let us assume that your house mortgage is $100,000 and you have a payment of $500 a month. You have not been able to pay your note for the past 4 months giving an arrearage of $2000 plus late fees.

Now that the mortgage company has decided to accelerate the mortgage, they essentially want you to write them a check for $100,000 or at least $2,000 to reinstate the mortgage; that is the meaning of the acceleration letter. Now at this point, you really are still in a workable position, because you could call the mortgage company and plead with them to accept two payments as a down payment, and then one and one half payments for the duration of the loan.

If not, then the attorney will proceed with the foreclosure. In the state of Michigan, there must be a thirty-day window between notification of the foreclosure and the actual sheriff sale. You will have another thirty days and, as I told you earlier, this still leaves ample time to save your house, that is, if that is what you want.

I have had clients come to me, explaining that they tried to set up arrangements and the bank accepted the compromise, but they just could not come up with the monies. This goes back to God, maybe this is outside His will. There are times when God simply decides that He wants you to do something different, and moves things and events to cause this necessary change in your life. I have always noticed that when I have had to move heaven and earth to get something done, then maybe it really was not what God wanted me to do in the first place. Now this does not mean when things are hard, just give up. It means that we do our very best, and God does the rest and, if we wind up in a place other than where we thought we should be, it may just be a result of the will of God.

I remember years ago, one our good friend was behind on his car note, and the company wanted to repossess it. He borrowed money from me, and then two days later, borrowed from my husband as well, trying to catch up his notes, but they repossessed the car anyway, it just was not, meant to be.

Years later, this man of God reflected on the incident and said that it was the best thing that ever happened to him, because he was doing a lot of things he had no business doing, going places he had no business going, and had he stayed on that path, he would have surely wound up in jail, or worse. He summed it all up, "Thanks be unto God".

If you've done, all that you can and still are unable to reinstate your mortgage, fear not because that does not have to be your last home. The attorney will then motion the sheriff's department to add the house to the list for sale, and they will then send you a letter informing you of the sale date. You will then have up until that date to get the mortgage company the arrearage as mentioned above.

Once the sheriff's sale is completed, you will have six months to live in the house, called a period of redemption. Redemption is a state-given provision, (remember each state is different), that allows you six months to sale the property for the balanced owed. You can sale the house or refinance the house, but if your credit is not strong enough, then refinance may not be an option.

During those six months, you can stay in the house, but if you move out of the house, and it appears that the house is abandoned, the redemption period, will be reduced down to 30 days. So be careful to keep the porch free of newspapers, keep the lawn cut, so that you won't give the wrong impression.

A client called me who was in her second month of redemption and stated that she had just come back from a two-week vacation, and there was a pad lock on her front door. She wanted to know what she could do, she thought that she had six months. She did, and this was really an illegal eviction, so I urged her to hang up the phone with me, and call the police and inform them of an illegal eviction.

The police came out and removed the lock from her door. She then called the real estate company that had placed a sign in her yard and informed them that they were violating her rights with an illegal eviction, and if they had persisted in their illegal actions, she would file a suit against them.

The real estate company, which was hired by the mortgage company, backed off, and we were able to sale the house, giving her cash with which to move, prior to the end of her redemption. This is the importance of understanding your rights.

In a similar situation, the real estate company placed a pad lock on the door, and removed some of the homeowner's belongings. The client called the police and the mortgage company, as well as a lawyer and sued the real estate company for illegal eviction, and child endangerment. When the real estate company illegally entered the premises, the owner's retarded daughter, hid in a closet. When they left and placed a pad lock on the door, unknowingly locking her in the house, they endangered her life. This in itself is a serious criminal offense, and the court agreed with the owner of the house.

To avoid these unfortunate scenarios, I cannot encourage you enough to be sure that you do not move out of the house, until you are ready to take all of your things, and until then be sure to keep the house in the same condition as you did when you had a mortgage on it.

10

Stop the Sale

"A leper pleads with Jesus, if you want to, you can heal me. Jesus says I want to…and instantly the disease disappears" Matthew 8:3-4

Repayment Plans are short-term methods with the mortgage company that allows you to keep you home, and make your payment with a small payment tacked on to cover the arrearage. The plan is generally set for six months, so if you are three months behind, and the amount of the mortgage is $400 a month, you therefore are behind $1200.

The $1200 is then broken up over 6 months therefore taking your payment from $400 to $600 per month. You need to ask your mortgage company so that you can make arrangements for you to participate in this program and therefore save your home. You will never know if you do not ask the question.

Loan Modification is a new offering from most mortgage companies. It allows the mortgage company to look at your arrearage, and your finances and determine a new rate that will allow them to place your arrearage on the back of your loan.

This option, may have been suggested, in one of the mortgage company's communications to you, you should call them and ask for their Hope department. They will want you to submit your pay stubs, and bank records, as well as a letter stating why you got behind in the first place.

Send up a smoke signal, and ask for help. Many times, you can ask your family and friends for help. A woman called me once and she said that her arrearage was only $3,000 and that she had called every person she knew, and asked them for a little money, $100 here, $200 there and that she only needed another $346 to pay off her arrearage. This is an excellent way to save your home. True you will feel nervous about asking for help, but you will feel even more nervous about asking people to help you move out of your home, so get over it.

Call your neighbors, your church, friends, co-workers, borrow from your credit cards or any place else that you think might not mind giving you a few bucks. You will find that the money will add up quickly, and the sooner you start, the sooner you will be on your way to the mortgage company's attorney to pay off your arrearage, and get your account in good standing.

Remember that without identifying the root, you will not know what else to change, and you could quickly be in the same position, and this time people are not going to be as accommodating in helping you out.

Selling off an Asset is a method used by one of my friends. She had discovered the root to her problem, trusting someone else to handle the day-to day affairs of her small business. Her business was doing very well, and she decided to allow her manager to handle the affairs as she embarked on other options.

Her managing employee then found it very easy to begin stealing the revenues, leaving her to pay the bills. She allowed this situation to exist for a year, before she got rid of the manager, and took on the job of managing her business.

Soon she found that the business was in fact very profitable, but she still needed to bring her mortgage current. She took one of her company vehicles, and sold it at auction. The proceeds from the auction, were used to reinstate the mortgage, and she today is able to stay on top of her mortgage, as she continues to manage her own business.

This method worked for her because she first looked in the mirror, to see what was out of line. She stood, in front of that mirror, asking herself, "Where do I need to make changes?" Many times as small business owners, we mistakenly think that the people hired to work for us, will be as concerned about the well-being of our business as we do.

We also think that we are somehow "joined" to our employees, but we are not. In reality, we must constantly look and see that they are doing what we hired them to do. Many times those people we hired sit at their desk all day, are not accomplishing a darn thing. They sit there sucking up coffee and donuts, playing on the internet, just waiting for their check, not having done anything to ensure that they contributed to the monies that back up that check.

I too have experienced those types of employees, and my human nature told me to give them another chance. While I 'm giving them another chance, my company was not making money, and on top of that they were spending hours on the phone talking to everybody in their family instead of doing their job. So then, you pay them, and pay them and after a while, you cannot even pay yourself. Get rid of any dead weight. You can hardly be a benefit to anyone, if you cannot take care of yourself.

Once you have gotten rid of the dead weight, find something that you can sell to raise the monies you need to get back on track. Sell some stock, cash out your IRA, sell extra vehicles at the auction, have a yard sell, and get rid of some other things, you can always replace them later. You know what you have in your house, basement, and garage, so sell something; this is no time for pride.

Chapter 13 Bankruptcy is an option, but many homeowners who seek this method wind up stopping the sale of the property, but if they have not applied some other methods in identifying the source, or the root of their problem, after a while they are unable to make the payments to the trustee.

Please understand that even though the bankruptcy laws were changed in 2005, you can still use that method to keep your home, provided you file prior, even if only the day before the sheriff sale.

The Bankruptcy Chapter 13 method provides a court order that forces the mortgage company to accept the payments of your current mortgage amount, plus a payment on the arrearage, (monies owed from the past months). You will complete a plan that states how much of the arrearage you will include with your monthly payment, and then make that entire payment directly to the trustee. Missing one payment will cause the trustee to dismiss the case, and you will be back where you were in the state of foreclosure.

If you plan to use this method, you should also be working on an independent plan that will allow you to pay the arrearage off in whole at the end of a certain period. In other words, let us say that through prayer you identified your purpose, and through prayer started working toward attaining it, while working your other job.

If the new venture is going well, rather than taking the extra money and buying a new car, or flat screen T.V., you would take that extra money and set it aside. Once you have all of the monies for the reinstatement, (you can obtain that figure from the mortgage company's attorney), you can submit the amount to the attorney's office, and then dismiss your bankruptcy case.

This method is best utilized once you have identified the root of your problem, and are working toward attaining this new goal, and therefore will have monies to both pay the trustee, while setting aside monies for the reinstatement.

Why not just stay in the bankruptcy? You could just stay within the Chapter 13 for the entire period of time; your attorney will stretch out the terms to 3 or 5 years. But on the other hand the mortgage company is not going to report you current until they receive the monies from the arrearage, so in the case of the bankruptcy at the end of the 3 or 5 years, or when you pay it off through the attorney.

Personally, I want to be current as quickly as possible, as I am in trouble in the first place from not doing what I should have in the beginning. Now that I have identified my "root", I want to get out of debt as soon as possible.

My goal is to pay my house off, so that all I am concerned about each year are my property taxes, and insurance, but I will not go into that in this book. Pick up my copy of "How to Stop Robbing Peter" to get started on that path. After all, if all things are possible through Christ who strengthens me, which I know to be true, then anyone can go from foreclosure to "paid in full", with faith and perseverance.

11

Other Methods to Save your Home

"I have given you authority over all power of the Enemy..." Luke 10:19

During the redemption period, not only do you have the right to retain possession and stay in the house, but you also have a right to sell the property. The only restriction is that the sell price must be equal too or greater than the balance of your original mortgage, outstanding taxes, water, and closing cost. All monies over and above this amount go to you, less any commissions for the sale.

If you really want to save your home, you will use that information for ammunition. Now if you know that you cannot afford to pay off the balance of the house to retain it, and we also know that you cannot get an additional loan, or can refinance the property, we sell the property to get rid of the mortgage company.

What if you sold your house to someone who could obtain financing, and then leased it, paying that person a note until you could get refinancing in your own name?

As I stated earlier, in order for you to obtain financing after your foreclosure, you will need to rent or lease a house for about 24 to 36 months, allowing the foreclosure on your credit report to heal. The bank will want to see that consecutive monthly rental history before considering you for a new mortgage.

To use this method, find someone who is looking for an investment, in which they can walk away with $5,000 in exchange for holding a mortgage on your house for 24 to 36 months. You will of course, need to put this contract in writing. You can look on line for a lease-option agreement, and you should consult an attorney.

In your contract, you should include a statement that allows you to make all payments directly to the mortgage company. The taxes and insurance should also be included in this new note. This ensures that the mortgage company does in fact receive the monies you are sending, avoiding any miscommunications.

The very best arrangement is to make all of your payments via check or money order, including the account number, payable to the mortgage company. Send that payment to the investor's address. The investor then has only to resend the payment to the mortgage company. He knows that you have paid the payment, and you know that the mortgage company received the payment.

I am asking that you take this kind of precaution because of a case in which an older woman who had been sick in the hospital for a very long time and subsequently got behind on her house notes. By the time she was better, and released from the hospital, the mortgage company was threatening foreclosure. She had filed a bankruptcy the year before, and therefore could not use that method, and the mortgage company refused to allow her any other option than paying the total reinstatement.

She had no way to come up with the total amount of the arrearage, and even though her house was worth 60% more than the mortgage balance, she did not qualify for refinancing.

She asked an investor to assist her by buying her house. Investors were constantly all looking to buy distressed properties, with guaranteed tenants. I approached one and she decided it was a good deal as the old lady only owed 40% of the value of the house.

The investor was interested because of the low balance on the house, and if the old woman reneged on the payments, the investor could always sell the house, recouping his investment from the profits.

The investor, bought the house for $5,000 more, than what the old lady owed her mortgage company and then entered into an agreement to lease the property back from the investor for 24 months.

In the original agreement they did not indicate that the payments should be made payable to the mortgage company, and so the old lady made her payments in cash to the new land holder. Things went well for about 16 months, and then the old lady received a letter in the mail indicating that the note had not been paid in three months, and that the house was going into foreclosure. The old lady immediately contacted the land holder. Long story short, the landholder had gotten behind on some other properties, and used the old woman's money to pay on those mortgages instead of sending in her payments to the mortgage company that was supposed to get them. Thirty days later the mortgage company did foreclose, and six months later put the old woman out on the street, in spite of the fact that she herself had never missed a payment.

Moral to the story, remember that we are all human. If you are in a vulnerable state, at least protect yourself as best you can. Had the old woman given the investor money orders made payable to the mortgage company, the investor would have had no choice but to pay the note.

This occurrence has happened many times in other situations as well. It seems that not until people are victimized, do they start asking the questions that should have been asked, initially. There are tons of folks, who have rented properties and wound up in the same situation. They paid their rents on time each month, and for whatever reason the landlord never paid the mortgage, or the taxes.

I mention taxes because there are a great many houses lost every year to the tax foreclosure. Many people who do not have their taxes included in their mortgage are subject to paying the taxes independently. Subsequently, they think that the tax payment is not that important, but what they don't understand is that the county can and will take the house for delinquent taxes two years old.

Each March, counties across the country prepare for a huge tax sale, notifying the residents of the pending foreclosure. Some years they have so many properties to auction off, that it takes two weeks to complete the whole matter.

If your house is contained in the tax sale, you have up until the day of the sale to redeem your property, pay off the taxes. The county will send you notice stating that you have until March, prior to the September sale, but if you call them up, and humbly communicate your intention, you generally will be able to go down and pay the bill, and retain your property.

Back to the lease back option, when you create your leaseback document, you will not only have a down payment amount, and the monthly payments, but the balance of the mortgage will be contained in a balloon. This balloon is due at the end, of the agreement and allows you to pay the balance of the house, once you obtain your new refinancing and therefore buy the house back from them by the end of the 3 years at the latest. Remember you are starting your purchase at the end of the 24 months so you have an additional year for the actual purchase.

Let me give you an example; you owe $50,000.00 on you original mortgage, and your house is worth $100,000.00. You want an investor to buy-out the old mortgage company so you sell the house to the new investor for $60,000.00.

At closing the title company will pay $50,000.00 to the old mortgage company, take about $3,500.00 for the closing cost of the transaction, and give you a check for $6,500.00. You in turn lease the property, with the option to purchase from the new landholder, paying them $5,000.00 for the option.

The new land-holder's mortgage is $450.00 a month, and that is the amount that you pay to that landlord, remembering to make the check payable to the new mortgage company. At the end of the 24 months, you still will only have paid interest on the loan. In case you do not know it, the first 20 years of a 30-year mortgage, pays nothing more than the interest with every payment.

Since you have only paid interest on the loan, you should probably have a payoff of $60,000.00, and that is the amount of the balloon. When you repurchase the house back from the landholder, your purchase price will be the $60,000.00.

This method has worked to help people retain their homes, but you must remember all that we discussed earlier regarding God's will for the situation. If God is against it, this will not work for you.

Another method is through the retention program with your mortgage company. Because there are so many homes in trouble today, almost every mortgage company has created a department with the explicit purpose of helping you to save your house and your credit.

Generally, what happens is the mortgage company will look at your financial situation and together you will determine what amount you can pay, and apply the arrearage to the end of the loan, allowing you to resume making current payments. Some of the mortgage companies will even go so far as to take your arrearage and place it on the end of your loan, and bring you current. You will not know this unless you ask. You must communicate with the mortgage company; there is no way around it, except through foreclosure.

12

Cash Out Before You Move Out

"...Lord who generously gives his riches to all those ask him for them" Romans 10:12

I want to reiterate that during redemption in some states like Michigan, you will have six months and, during that time, you will not make any mortgage or property insurance payments because that all is now the burden of the mortgage company. Check with your state and see how much time you would have after the sheriff's sales.

I, however, encourage you to obtain a renter's policy, just in case, to cover the loss of any possessions that could be lost in a fire, or some other incident.

During redemption, so long as you maintain possession, no one can evict you, but many may try to pressure you to leave, not realizing that you know your rights. The real estate company that is hired by the mortgage company will offer you a "cash for keys" exchange in an attempt to get you out of that house as early as possible.

The keys for cash program works like this, you move all of your belongings out of the house, including all debris, and vacuum floors so that the house is completely bare and the mortgage company will then give you the money. But be careful, if every piece of furniture, including the appliances are not moved out of the house they will not pay you the money.

One of my clients tried that process and she as a single mother, moved out almost everything she could, but was unable to move one piece of large furniture. The real estate company did not pay her the $2000 that they had promised her, so be careful.

The bank has no choice but to allow you the six months, but at the end, they will ask you to move. You do not have to move on the final day of redemption unless, of course, that is what you choose to do, and that would mean that you have located your temporary setting. We will talk about that later in this discussion.

Once your redemption is over, the mortgage company then needs to take possession and, by law, they can only do this through the court. The only entity that can evict you is the sheriff's department, and they will not do that without an order from the court. At the end of the redemption, you could move or you could wait for them to evict you. About a week after redemption is over the mortgage company will file a motion to evict with the county courthouse.

The court will contact you, with a notice that says either move by this date or come to court. Go to court, ask the judge to give you an extra 30 days, in most situations the judge will allow the extension.

The judge is sensitive to the fact that you have just lost your home, and will try to help you by being as fair as the law will allow. Jesus told us "to ask and you shall receive". He also said, "You don't have because you won't ask", so ask the judge and he will give you more time.

Please understand the letter from the court is the second most important paper, after the intent to foreclosure, in the entire process. If you do not respond and show up at the court, the judge will have no choice but to sign a writ for you to move within 7 days. So go to court.

Once you find your final date to move, you should start planning and packing. There is nothing worst than trying to organize a move at the last minute. Your goal is to find a place that you can easily afford to rent for 24 months. We will talk more about this important step to getting a new home in the next chapter.

While you are packing, which is an overwhelming endeavor within itself, you should purge things as you go along. You are about to start a brand new journey so use this opportunity to get rid of as much junk as possible. Take as much stuff to the Salvation Army as you can bear to give away. They will gladly take things and give you a receipt for the donation in the meanwhile.

One other important tip is the storage of the things you intend to keep. When we moved we contacted a company called P.O.D.'s, which provides portable storage units. They brought us a unit that resembled a railroad car, placing it in our driveway. We then loaded our belongings into the car, and once complete they picked it. They then stored it at their facility until we were ready to move into your new place.

When I moved, I planned to stay with my mom until I could purchase my home, so the POD with all of my belongings stayed at the facility yard, which I could visit at any time to get things out if I needed. When we finally closed on our home, they brought my units and placed them right in the driveway. We took about a week to get all the things out, and about 3 weeks to get it loaded initially. There was no extra cost, and it made the whole move much easier.

When you finally have finished removing your things from the house, you want to make contact with the real estate company and give them the keys. This is important as it prevents the local crack heads coming through and stripping the house of its pipes, and fixtures. Believe me they will come through quicker than you would believe.

Lastly, say a prayer thanking God for the time you spent in his house, and ask His will be done as you move forward to your next home, close the door and do not look back.

13

Don't forget about the IRS

"Give to Caesar what is his, and give God everything that belongs to God"
Matthew 22:21

Let's say that you have done the above, you have prayed and communicated, but still are unable to find a solution, or you simply don't have the funds available to make a compromise with the mortgage company, or you simply choose to give up, well then let's discuss the best possible way to surrender.

First of all do not just move out in the middle of the night, the bank will consider that you have abandoned the property, and then worst of all, the local jokers will come in and strip the house down, making it harder for the bank to sell the property. This is bad for all involved, including you, because even though they take the house in sheriff's sale, you still owe them the difference between what it auctions for and what you owe, plus attorney fees, back taxes, and other foreclosure transactional fees.

One of my rental properties was literally "stripped", down to the bone, two days after the tenants moved out. The moved out one day, and at about 9 pm when it was too dark to finish, they locked up the house and called me to meet them in the morning, so that I could be there when they finished to get the key.

Well, 9am the next morning, 12 hours later, we both arrived at the house at the same time to find that not only were their remaining boxes, and sofa missing, but so were the doors, windows, furnace, fixtures, metal bars of the windows and doors, as well as half of the vinyl siding off the back of the house.

Had this house been in foreclosure, the "damaged value" would have been reduced so low, that even after the sale, the remaining balance would be 70% of the original balance. The vandalism, which the mortgage company is not going to repair, reduces the sale price at sheriff sale to $5,000, leaving me with huge balance.

This happens all too often, and generally, the house is boarded-up, which then becomes a haven for drug dealers, crack-heads, and worst.

When a house is boarded-up, it reduces the value of the other homes in the neighborhood. Remember you reap what you sow, so "do care" about the neighborhood even after you have moved out. Do your best to protect it, don't abandon your home.

Okay if that didn't impress you then consider this, why not get some cash out before you move out. That's right, cash out.

Remember, I told you that the mortgage company still holds you responsible for the property, whether you abandon it or not. Well so does Uncle Sam, what's more, he wants to get paid, for the privilege of you owning the house.

The IRS will consider your foreclosure as income, so you need to be sure and cover yourself accordingly. I never understood just how the IRS considers this as income, but the important thing to know is that they will, so they will calculate the amount that you owe them, based on the difference between the market value and what you owe.

In my case, we owed $130,000 on our house at the time of foreclosure. When the house sold at auction it was worth $180,000, therefore, the IRS considered that we earned $50,000 and because of the monies my husband already earned from his job, they increased our tax rate, and we owed an additional $20,000 in taxes. Now if you have ever dealt with the IRS you know that come hell or high water they will get their money. They will go into your bank accounts, garnish your paychecks, and do whatever is necessary to get the money owed. This is one debt, that you simply cannot walk away from, or ignore, thinking that it will simply go away, because it will not.

Now if you go to a normal tax preparer they will probably be inexperienced in the proper filing of a return with a foreclosure attached. There are certain precautions that must be addressed, in order to get rid of the foreclosure tax debt. If you go to the IRS web site and review their information on Capital Gains, you will find a workable solution.

The Capital Gain gives you a break, up to $250,000 per two years, so long as you lived in the property, prior to foreclosure. This point is important; you must have resided in the property, in order to take advantage of this option.

So what does this do for you? Simple, it will erase the income from the foreclosure and thereby reduce your taxes back to the original state. If you were due a refund of $700 before the foreclosure bill was slapped on your credit, then you will receive that amount in refund. It is important that you address this issue, as we are trying to rebuild your credit so that you can buy another house not to far down the road.

How far down the road really is up to you. I mean many mortgage companies would like to see 24 to 36 months before, they feel that you are worthy of a mortgage. That is if you have also created other new credit in the meantime, but we will get into that in the next chapter.

14

Rebuilding After the Foreclosure

"I make all things new" Revelations 21:5

The most important fact that you must consider is that this is not your last house. God owns all the houses, and if you remain obedient, you will soon find yourself in a far better house, wondering why you were ever scared. Please understand that life is what you make it. So, if you want a new house, then you can move in that direction with just four little ingredients; planning, prayer, propensity, and persistence.

Everything needs a plan in order for it to be successful. The Bible is full of God's plans and specific directions for success. Even Solomon in all his wisdom, had a plan that detailed, to the letter how the Lord's temple had to be built, and precisely how much materials were required for its completion.

I encourage you, to take a look at Solomon's plans, it's amazing how detailed they are. God instructed him to the letter, the exact number of laborers needed, what they should be paid, the materials to be used, on and on.

By taking the time to plan, Solomon had a good idea of exactly how God's temple, which he built only for the glory of the Lord, would come out. He did not just guess, or do things as he went along. No, he took the time to outline a plan that would lead him to his destination.

My mom reminds me that you can't keep putting in the same things and expecting the outcome to be different. So what did you not do, that allowed you to loss your house? Did you have an adequate job that paid you a reasonable salary? Did you buy a house that you could not afford, and then fail to find a way to earn that extra money you needed to keep it? Or were you simply a victim of life, your spouse died and you could not make the payments?

You must cause change in your life. You must find a way to be in the position, so that when God makes the way, you can receive the blessings. Understand that God will help you, leading you all the way, if you trust Him, and heed to the sound of His voice. He will even send angels to aid you, and before long, you will be on your path.

I once asked my mom when she knew that she was to take the path of nursing. She smiled and explained that she originally had planned to go to school only to fulfill the requirements to open a day care service. She was taking classes, when she met a young lady, who convinced my mom, to go with her to a seminar on nursing programs, with guaranteed financial aide. She went and became interested in the program as there was a shortage of nurses. Therefore they were trying to do whatever, to train more nurses.

What did we just learn? That effort, will always be met, and God will make a way, but you must trust Him, and never forget that he works through other people. You never know when you are in the company of angels, so be nice to everyone, and listen for messages.

Related to the topics discussed earlier, yes everything does flow through the Lord, so what lesson did you learn from your foreclosure?

Because you are a Child of God, bad things will come, but you must go through. The difference is that you know where to turn when trouble comes. That does not mean that you set back and let life direct you, but rather you need to live life abundantly.

To live that abundant life, you need a successful plan. A good plan starts with a goal. This goal, is the end result, that you expect from your plan. Think of it this way, your plan is just like a roadmap.

So let's say you were traveling to West Haven, Texas. I don't know how to get there but a map quest will create a route that allows me to get there showing every road, and exit and turn necessary. Fortunately it will even detail the approximate time it will take to get there.

Well, your plan will do just the same thing, and if you are realistic in your estimations, and diligent in your efforts you will obtain your goals, within the expected time.

So let's start at the beginning, you want to save your home or buy a new one, you should first make a list of all the things you want.

I encourage you to write it out in detail, and then put it away somewhere where you can look at it at least twice a year. You will look at it whenever you feel overwhelmed, or under stress, and then you will look at it again once you get your home, and if you are like me you will have gotten almost everything on your list.

Let's start from the beginning, and develop a budget. You will be surprised how much more control you will have over your finances with a budget. You must control your money and not let the money control you. I remember when my mood, and everything was controlled, by my bank account.

The real problem was that I was not paying attention to my money. Actually, I was making so much money, on a regular basis that I did not take the time to count and keep track of it until the money ran out.

I would know when it was time to deposit more money because a check would bounce. I did not realize that the bank makes mistakes as well. I did not know that many times those mistakes act like one big domino, and cause a whole bunch of mess.

I remember once I made two deposits at the same bank into two different accounts. One deposit was in cash the other a certified check. The check was a rather large one about 5 times as much as the cash deposit.

I wrote the payroll for my employees against the large account a week later knowing that a certified check required about 48 hours to clear. Much to my surprise the checks bounced. All of them, I was nervous as I cat as I called the bank manager and he said that the bank had no record of the deposit. He asked if I still have the deposit ticket.

Rushing to the bank, I gave him the deposit ticket for my actual deposit and the smaller one in the other account as well. He was able to locate the small cash deposit, but the larger one did not appear on the cashiers tape for that day. I had to wait almost 20 days before the bank could acknowledge the deposit. Every since that day, I have been hard on myself about keeping up with the bank balance, and making sure that what I put in the bank gets to my account.

So, the "new you" will keep track of your bank balance. You will also try, and avoid the use of credit cards. No cash, no purchase. Credit is one of the biggest traps for the uneducated consumer, and it is something that you should use sparingly. I realize that you need credit for the purchase of your house, and car, but that is not the extent, your credit is used in determining your car insurance, and more and more items so let's get an understanding of exactly when you should use your credit cards.

You do not use them for consumption. Consumption is something that is used up, like dinner. Think about it unless you are paying off the dinner at the end of the month, like in the instance of reimbursement for your job, you do not want to pay for a dinner 4 months down the road. By the time the bill comes, you won't even remember what you ate. So let's try and pay our dinner bills in cash, while we are in the repositioning phase of this life.

Put those credit cards away. We want to get the bill paid down, and therefore you must stick to a cash basis only. If you don't have the cash to pay for something, chances are you don't need it.

I further discuss these topics in my, "How to Stop Robbing Peter to pay Paul" journey. These are important matters, after all it's up to you to control your money, not let it control you.

15

Planning for Prosperity

"The Lord will bless...and prosper everything you do when you arrive in the land the Lord your God is giving you" Deuteronomy 28:8

On the other side of the foreclosure is a plan for your new future. You have decided what it is you want to do, you will next make a plan to get you there. When I decided that I wanted to get a new home, I had to make a plan that ended in a new home. I first looked at my credit. Aside from the foreclosure, I had to look at the other negative or positive things on my credit report. So step one was to request my credit report.

When I reviewed my credit report, I found many entries that did not belong to me, and should not have been on my credit report in the first place. To get rid of them I sent written complaints to the credit bureau to have the inaccuracies removed. I simply wrote a brief letter to the credit bureau, requesting that they remove the inaccurate information. This is a right that many of us overlook, and allow incorrect information to pull our credit scores down.

You should also look at the overall balances owed on each account. In the past, I found errors in that section as well. I contacted the creditors and they updated the information. When reviewing for balances note the low ones, you will be surprised how a small $50 debt can bring down your credit rating. So pay it and get rid of it.

Getting rid of the large negative accounts on your credit report, can be completed in different ways; pay it off, negotiation, and last result bankruptcy. Bankruptcy, Chapter 7 should be used as a last ditch effort, of which you should be prepared prior to filing, as with everything else you need to have a plan for rebuilding your credit prior to filing.

The second method is to negotiate with the creditor. You will be surprised how many creditors would just as soon settle the delinquent account for 60% of less. I have even used this process with short sales on properties. The method is rather simple, but does involve you speaking directly with a representative from the company.

You will tell them that you are still unable to satisfy the debt, but if they could accept 50% of the balance owed, you could send them a check within the next 10 days. In my experience, the creditor will turn down your initial offer, and counter with one of their own. Once you get them to the rock bottom amount that they will accept, you then want to be sure that they will comply with your demand. Your demand is that they mark the account paid, and then close the account, thereby no longer marring your credit report with negative marks.

The third method is to acquiesce or pay the amount owed in full. I would not try this method unless I had money to burn, I would first try and get them to settle the bulk of the debt before I do anything else.

If you choose method two or three, be sure and get a letter stating that the debt has been satisfied, and no other monies are due with regard to that account. This is a vital step, as they can come back to haunt you later.

I recently had a client that I walked through in liquidating her home. We did our due diligence, and found an old debt, she claimed was paid, years ago. I told her to bring a copy of the satisfaction of debt letter to the closing so that she could give it to the title company. Well she could not locate the document and further the bank that held the lien against her property had since sold the debt to an outside collection company.

The title company could not simply take her word that the debt was paid, and she had no evidence of her payment. So, the title company had no choice but to honor the collection company's interest.

The amount was $10,000 and was almost half of what she was to walk away with at closing. The woman was upset, but could hold on to the property no longer has it was involved in a foreclosure transaction.

My non-profit stepped in and prepared an offer to the collection company, which they accepted for $6,000.00. This was better than paying $10,000.00, so she accepted the terms of the negotiation. She would not have had to pay the amount had she retained her evidence. This is an example of the importance of organization. Keep your things in order, don't get rid of cancelled checks, until you are sure they are no longer beneficial. Always keep your journals, because as in this case she could have found the payment in her check journal, and contacted the bank for a copy of the cancelled check.

Once you have identified all of the folks on your credit report, sorting through which are accurately listed as your debt, and you have removed the debts that do not belong to you, there will still be one big debt.

The mortgage company, will show a difference between what was owed, and the amount that they actually sold the property. This balance is your responsibility, and it is up to you to arrange to pay the debt.

You have two choices, you can either schedule a repayment plan, thereby paying the entire amount owed over a period of time, directly with that lender, or you can try to file a Chapter 7, which will wipe away the whole thing. You should be sure and plan for that as well. Talk to a lawyer, but keep in mind you can still use bankruptcy to help get your finances in order.

When I say, "plan for your bankruptcy", I mean that you should have a workable plan, which details why you are filing bankruptcy, what you will achieve, as well as the steps you will use to rebuild your credit once the bankruptcy is discharged.

Today's bankruptcy laws provide that you attend consumer credit counseling courses prior to your filing. When I filed, I knew that I wanted to get back to the point where I could buy a house, and a car. I also knew that beyond the things on my credit report, I had to show that I was a suitable credit risk. I knew that in order to qualify for a mortgage, I would need to show 24 to 36 months of rental history. I would also need to show that same amount of bank statements.

So prior to my filing bankruptcy I leased a home, and arranged with the owner to wire my payments, therefore I satisfied both of the above stated requirements, because I could order a copy of my bank statements. The wire transfer would appear, because I put the word "Rent" in the memo line of the transfer document.

The court discharged the debt, and I had the task of rebuilding my credit. To accomplish that goal, I first requested two secured credit cards. I was very careful, to never charge more than 40% of the available credit.

This method helped to quickly raise my credit score. After 6 months of paying my credit bill on time, paying only the minimum payment each month, and making my rent payment on time I was able to apply for a car loan.

Let me digress for one moment, with regard to the credit cards, it is imperative that you not max out your credit card each month. Many think that it is ok to max out the credit card, as long as you pay it off at the end of the month. The practice only works with accounts such as American Express, where payment of the entire bill is required each month.

Visa and MasterCard are different as they require you to pay a minimum payment, but when the credit agency calculates your score they are not only looking at whether or not you pay your bill on time each month. They look at how much available credit you leave on your cards each month. In other words, they want to see that you use a small amount of your available credit each month, and make at least your minimum payment when required.

After a while, not as long as you think, you will be able to buy another home. Be sure to get what you want, after all you have to work hard to afford it, but be sure that you are in line with your ability to pay for it as well. Like I said earlier, order my the next step entitled, “How to Stop Robbing Peter”, and let’s talk about enjoying a “paid in full” life.

16

Final Thoughts

"Fear God and obey his commandments, for this is the entire duty of man" Ecclesiastes 12:13

Many of the things I have talked about, I have had to learn on my own, in that great school of hard knocks. Although most of the information can be found in various places, you should receive bits and pieces of information in the pile of junk mail that immediately follows the public recording of the intent to foreclosure. No one was able to teach me these things, because I had to learn the truth for myself. When you are standing in the dark, everything seems like a lie, even the truth.

Seek truth and share it with your children, remember that God assigned you to them, and part of your purpose is to point them in the way of truth. Yes, they have to find their own way, as you did, but it is up to you to give them a head start. Teach them the way of truth early. Make them obey you, so that they will understand how to obey God. Give them positive life experiences; show them places and things that will challenge their minds. Make sure that they know high school is but the beginning, and that college is a necessity.

Establish some interest bearing accounts that can allow you to set aside monies for their education. The cost of college is staggering at best, and is subject to go up each year. Yes, your children should apply for financial aide, but in between the gap of what they will get and what you will owe, is the amount you planned to set aside before they could even begin to talk.

You want your child to attain the life that God intended, and with technology today, it is almost impossible for your child to be successful without a college degree. We are to live an abundant life, as Jesus teaches us. You must do all that you can to be sure that your children have access to all the tools that will help propel them to such a position. This position will allow them to easily pay their tithes, taxes, bills and still have much to give away.

This is a form of love. This is the way God loves us. He wants the very best for us, and if we follow his plan, he allows our cups to run over with blessings. We must be sure and love our children in the same way. Not just with our lips, but in our actions.

Many people mistake love for the passion, and sex as portrayed on television, but love is much more than those surface things. To quote a great author

"Love is patient, love is kind. It does not envy, it does not boast, it is not proud. It is not rude, it is not self-seeking, it is not easily angered, and it keeps no record of wrongs. Love does not delight in evil but rejoices with the truth. It always protects, always trusts, always hopes, and always perseveres. Love never fails. But where there are prophecies, they will cease; where there are tongues, they will be stilled; where there is knowledge, it will pass away. For we know in part and we prophesy in part, but when perfection comes, the imperfect disappears. .And now these three remain: faith, hope and love. But the greatest of these is love" (1 Corinthians 13:4-7).

Love somebody else today, give someone a smile, whisper into a stranger's ear, the truth that, "God loves you". You don't know what they may be going through, or where they are in the "through" part of going.

They might just be in foreclosure as well, and need to understand that it is only a test, that will eventually pass away, and all will be well if they trust in the Lord. Avoid being so caught up in your own problems, that you can't muster up a smile to someone else.

At another time in my life when I was going through much turmoil, the Lord whispered to me that I must find a way to love anyway. That was when I started my non-profit and personally provided housing to the homeless. Feeding them out of my own pockets without expecting anything in return, I was able to love, and it made my going through all the easier. It was like a spoon full of sugar, and the medicine went down without a gag.

My children were by my side the whole time, and it really felt great lending my time and talents to those who needed them, surely it was better than sitting around "mooping" in self-pity. I mention that my kids were apart of it because I want to be sure that I give them as much of me as possible.

As I grow, I want them to grow, and come to understand many of the things that took me 40 years to learn. I encourage you to do the same for your children. That means helping them to understand their place in the world as it applies to their relationship with God.

Encourage your children to develop their own relationship with God, helping them to tackle the huge concept of money. Helping them to understand money is only a tool, and as a tool, one must know its proper use in order to be successful.

They must realize their purpose in life, because life without purpose is a hard road to walk. Most importantly, help them to understand the power of love. You should teach them that God is love, and that they should have love in their heart for everyone regardless of what is going on around them.

Sometimes I wish that for one moment I had a huge P.A, system that allows everyone to hear my voice, and I would yell for the whole world to hear "If you know not love, you know nothing at all". Oh, I guess I just did.

That's all for now, so go save your house, and remember that through it all, God loves you. May peace be with you and your family.

About The Author

Born 1963, in Baltimore Maryland, and transplanted in 1967 to Detroit Michigan. Tris is a business owner directing non-profit projects that serve the needs of the homeless.

In 1995, she and her family moved to Atlanta Georgia, during which time she suffered many emotional hardships that eventually contributed to financial distress. It was during those hardships, which she considers her "wilderness experience" that she began to grow in her relationship with God.

During that time, she learned that the easiest way to get through emotionally trying periods, was to spend time helping others. At that time, she started working with a group of young adults and together they created alternative housing situations for the homeless.

In 2003, Tris and her family returned to her hometown in Michigan, and continued her work, helping others to grab hope, plant seeds, and pray answers into reality.

One of the main methods discovered was the use of information. Many of the people aided had no knowledge of their rights with regard to foreclosure, or bankruptcy. Many people didn't even know that they had to check behind the bank each month to be sure that their bank accounts were correct.

Having economic issues of her own, she prayed that God would make sense out of all of the various paths on which she had traveled. God continued to bless her, allowing her to travel around the world, and witness many different things. She now needed to be a vessel for God, and therefore do her part in directing others to locate the blessings in their own life's, regardless of circumstances.

Using her gifts, she began to write about the tests, and trials in her life. The accounts of her experiences, and how God continued to answer her prayers in the middle of tremendous storms, should serve as a proper means to encourage others. The result, thanks be unto God, are contained in the following books as of this printing:

"Options After Foreclosure"

"How to Stop Robbing Peter, to Pay Paul"

"Grow Your Own Fig Tree"

"Tales of the Marvelous Light"

"Chronicles of Love"

"How to Stop Robbing Peter, to Pay Paul" is a self- help tool that promotes living a "Paid in Full" life. It shows you how to establish a plan that ends in helping you become self-sufficient, happily living without debt. You will have full control of your monies, spending, and your life being prosperous as God intended.
Order today for only $10 at www.tradepostearth.com.

"Grow Your Own Fig Tree", by Tris
In order to live a prosperous life, one must work. God has to have something to bless. You must understand that the prayers are effective when you have placed a seed to grow. Your seed is your business, thereby providing a way around the unemployment issues that plague our economy. You will in fact create your own business. In this guide, we discuss just how easy it is to transform a hobby into a prosperous money making business. We also will introduce various businesses that are easy to start from home, and therefore help you to grow your very own Fig Tree.
Order today for only $10 at www.tradepostearth.com.

"Tales of the Marvelous Light", by Tris
This journey contains eyewitness accounts of God's angels at work in the life's of everyday people. It provides hope as you see God working in our life to guide us to the paths of safety, prosperity, and joy through true events. Written as a series of bedtime stories it is truly a treat for the reader.
Order today for only $10 at www.tradepostearth.com.

"Chronicles of Love", by Tris

This journal provides insight into the actions of men and women, describing how they seek the most valuable gift from God of all, "Love". It serves to unravel the complex matters by looking at true accounts of relationships, and helps the reader to understand the "how's" and "why's" of relationships.
Order today for only $10 at www.tradepostearth.com.

For more detail about these titles, as well as projects under development, please check out the publisher's page at MustardSeedWorks.com

All titles are available through
TradePostEarth.com at discounted price
Or at Amazon.com

Sponsors

I would like to thank my sponsors. Although I am thankful to God first, I acknowledge that He works through relationships, and the following people acting in their own obedience, helped in the finance of this project. I would like to take this opportunity to mention them by name, and publicly express my appreciation.

Paulett Griffin
Mr. & Mrs. Ozell Putman
Albert DeWalt
Rasha King
Charlie Black
William Tate Jr.
Dwayne Van
Donna Brown
Carolyn Presley
Mr. and Mrs. Andre Lowe
Mr. and Mrs. Michael Griffin
Carlos and Aluna Johnson
Brenda S. Jackson
Dr. & Mrs. Alex Pickens
Mr. & Mrs. Thomas Howard

QUICK ORDER FORM

Fastest method go to: www.TradePostEarth.com

Or call 800.738.7712

Email: tradepostearth@aol.com

Postal Orders: Trade Post Earth, P.O. Box 70, Franklin Michigan 48025 USA

Enclosed is my payment of $ _______. Please send me the following books.

☐ Stop Robbing Peter ☐ Grow Fig Tree
☐ Chronicles ☐ Marvelous Light

I understand that I may return any of them for a full refund—for any reason, no questions asked.

Please also send me FREE information on:

☐ Quantity Discounts ☐ Scheduling a Seminar

Name: ______________________________

Address: ______________________________

City: ______________ State: __________ Zip: _________

Telephone: ______________ Email: ______________

Sales tax: Please add 6% for products shipped to Michigan.

Corporate Sponsors

Special thanks to my friends at: